Postmodernism and Youth Ministry

Postmodernism and Youth Ministry

An Introduction

SCOTT M. KOPP

WIPF & STOCK · Eugene, Oregon

POSTMODERNISM AND YOUTH MINISTRY
An Introduction

Wipf & Stock
An Imprint of Wipf and Stock Publishers
199 W. 8th Ave., Suite 3
Eugene, OR 97401
www.wipfandstock.com

ISBN 13: 978-1-60899-352-9

Manufactured in the U.S.A.

To the students; past, present, and future;
of Archbishop Hoban High School, Akron, Ohio

Contents

Preface

THIS BOOK is a revision and expansion of my master's thesis, completed in April 2007 at Walsh University in North Canton, Ohio. As we all have, with my contacts in other schools, churches, and friendships; I have fallen into numerous ministry discussions that eventually turned to the subject of my studies. I have been struck by the number of ministers today that are unaware of the particulars, or even overall idea, of postmodernism, and how it affects our young people. With this in mind and with the encouragement of colleagues, I have decided to have this text published.

This book is written for all who work with youth and young adults in ministry; be they youth minister, youth pastor, director of religious education, Sunday school or P.S.R. teacher, high school or college campus minister, or pastor or pastoral associate. It is an introduction to postmodernism and a companion piece for ministry with postmodern youth. For a more complete overview of youth ministry as I believe it should look today, the best overall introduction and guide to comprehensive youth ministry is *Renewing the Vision: A Framework for Youth Ministry* by the United States Conference of Catholic Bishops (Washington, DC: United States Conference of Catholic Bishops, 1997).

As of this writing, I am celebrating my first decade of ministry in the Diocese of Cleveland and am currently in my eighth year as Campus Minister at Archbishop Hoban High School, a Catholic high school in Akron, Ohio, under the leadership of the Brothers of Holy Cross from Notre Dame, Indiana. I am a "cradle-Catholic," yet active in dialogue with people of other denominations and faith traditions. While the theology and emphasis in the writing is intended primarily for Roman Catholics, the concepts are broad enough to appeal to all Christian denominations.

I hope this book provides an understanding of postmodernism and its ramifications for your own ministry. May it be an opening for continued dialogue and an affirmation for you in your calling as a minister to the youth of today.

S.M.K.

Akron, OH

February 5, 2010

Acknowledgments

MY THANKS could run for pages when I reflect on all of the people who have helped me over the years, the students from whom I have learned, and the colleagues with whom I have worked. To simplify matters and to not leave anyone out, my thanks and gratitude go out to the institutions I have been a part of in my ministry and the key people that have guided me and supported me along the way.

First thanks to my family, from my mother that raised me in the faith, to Dad, Dave, and Michael. I love you all. A special word to my only brother Dave: no one understands me, challenges me, and supports me like you. The cake is a lie!

My everlasting appreciation and devotion to the Capuchin-Franciscan friars of the Pennsylvania Province of St. Augustine. You baptized me and taught me the faith at St. Joseph's Church in Dover, Ohio. You welcomed me into your community and formed me in my first steps as a minister. You continue to let me share in your life and charism. Pax et Bonum.

For all my friends and loved ones, especially the Kramer-Hohenberger family. Thank you for the years of peaceful weekend evenings, vacations, and free dinners. Thank you especially to Jen, John, Leah, and Mark for the use of your couches throughout graduate school and the writing of this book.

For the staff and parishioners of St. Anthony of Padua Church in Parma, Ohio. You gave me my first job in youth ministry, let me guide your children, and provided me space to begin reflecting on the meaning of contemporary youth and how to most effectively walk with them. I am forever grateful.

For Walsh University in North Canton, Ohio. I never cease to put the tools and education you gave me into practice. Thanks especially to my thesis advisor, Monsignor Lewis F. Gaetano, D.Min., and the Director of the Writing Center, Kathleen Buttermore.

For the community of Archbishop Hoban High School in Akron, Ohio, and all of the Brothers of the Congregation of Holy Cross. For close to ten years, I have rarely sprung out of bed not loving my job. The opportunities have been an adventurous blessing: with weekend retreats, summers volunteering with the handicapped, music ministry practices, canned food drives, talent shows, trips to Kentucky, Montreal, Mexico, and Ghana, and for all the general ways of making a fool of myself daily. I have been truly humbled and blessed to mentor your students. I am yours.

Finally, for Bradley and Ian. You bring joy to my heart.

Introduction

ENTERING THE world of youth can strike fear in many when they reflect on what they see on television and in the print media. It can also raise painful memories, for many, of our own difficult teenage years. It takes a certain type of person to choose youth ministry as a career. While many parishes may simply hire someone to "play with the kids" or gather a few volunteers to help with the youth group, effective youth ministry is a necessity and requires much more. My own experiences as a parish youth minister and currently as a Catholic high school campus minister color my view on this subject. I have been told that my job is not "real" ministry, that my job consists only of playing volleyball and planning picnics with kids, wandering the halls drinking coffee, and that I am not a "real" minister. The question continuously arises as to what I do all day. And yet parents and other supporters also provide praise for the difference we are making in their children's lives. These experiences, along with extensive studies in youth ministry during graduate school, and as part of a certification program, have led me to view youth ministry as a true calling and vocation in the church. Youth ministers cannot just be volunteers thrown into the position with no training or understanding of all that it entails.

Early in my graduate studies, I became aware of the concept of postmodernism. I had heard of it, but not in any way beyond art or philosophy and not in any great depth. As this particular class continued, I began to consider the impact that postmodernism has on the world of the youth with whom I minister. I believe there is an absolute need for youth and young adult ministers to understand the characteristics of postmodern culture in order to be effective ministers.

The normal developmental problems that we all encounter through adolescence have been affected and increased by the postmodern worldview. While for many still under the age of forty this is a shared worldview, the particulars of postmodernism have had a greater effect on the present generation. Sr. Sandra M. Schneiders, IHM, writes that "postmodernity is both a child of and a protest against modernity, which is itself a child of the Enlightenment."[1] "Modern" should not be confused with "contemporary." The Modern Age is a definite historic time period, beginning[2] with the Enlightenment and continuing today. The Enlightenment, beginning with Rene Descartes in the middle of the seventeenth century, was the "light" of reason, culture, and teaching after the supposed "darkness" of the Middle Ages. Postmodernity is the reaction to what was lacking in the modern mindset. Yet, as we will see, it is not a definite break from modernity, as it shares many of the same methods, processes, and assumptions. With its ori-

---

1. Schneiders, *Finding the Treasure*, 111.

2. "Beginning" is a problematic word, but easier to use in this context. The problem comes with pinpointing when the Middle Ages end: at the end of the fifteenth century? in 1517 with the Reformation? or in 1492 with Columbus? For the purposes of our study, let us agree that 1492 was a significant year and that by the Enlightenment we are definitely into the Modern Age.

gins in the art, architecture, and literature of the 1940s and 1950s,[3] postmodern culture is most closely associated with the children of the 1960s, the 1970s, and continues today. Many labels separate these groups, such as Generation X, Generation Y, the Millennials, etc; but they all in some way are affected by and are products of postmodern culture. "The bridge carrying children and youth from baptism to mature faith has become less and less effective."[4] The children within the postmodern generation need particular help in this transition; from adolescence and having their parents tell them to go to church, to an owned faith where they decide for themselves to be involved in the life of faith; and not all of the methods used in youth ministry are working. To help teens in this time of transition, the church not only needs to provide caring adults to mentor and guide them; it also needs qualified youth ministers trained in the demands of the present culture to provide meaningful and appropriate experiences for today's teens. A more thorough understanding of effective methods will lead to the overall improvement of youth ministry.

The world of today's youth appears to be a world unto itself; therefore, a proper understanding of what life within this world is like is a must for effective ministry. What speaks to the teen mind at this time of development creates the culture in which s/he feels the safest. The United States Conference of Catholic Bishops recognizes that "adolescents reflect a distinct age group and 'culture' within our society."[5] Youth is its own culture. Across ethnic, economic,

3. Inbody, "Postmodernism," 523.

4. Martinson, "Spiritual But Not Religious," para. 7.

5. U.S. Bishops, *Renewing the Vision*, 45.

and racial divisions; youth culture stands as a subculture within each.

When looking at the present culture, it is comforting to know that "we are not the first to engage in reform, revision, and innovation. We are not the first to witness the cultural terrain shift around us."[6] It happened with the transformation from an ancient, premodern worldview in the time up through the Roman Empire and the Middle Ages; and again at the dawn of the Modern Age. The Middle Ages is the time between the fall of the western Roman Empire and the beginning of the Modern Age, roughly 500 to 1500 AD. Premodern is the term we can apply now for the worldview that included both the ancient world and the Middle Ages. The Premodern Age, as opposed to the Modern, is marked by an emphasis on the other-worldly, the triumph of God or gods, and the subordination of the human to the divine. At the close of the Classical Age, the Church remained, retained, and promoted the focus on the divine and humanity's subordination. With the fall of "the Roman Empire in the late fifth century, the Church was the only institution in the Western world capable of dealing in any stabilizing way with the chaos that followed."[7]

The Second Vatican Council (1962–65) examined the Catholic Church's own history and place in the world with the "Pastoral Constitution on the Church in the Modern World", more commonly known by its Latin title "*Gaudium et Spes.*" *Gaudium et Spes* (which means "hope and joy") traces this understanding of its relevance within our present question: "The Church learned early in its history to

6. Carson, *Transforming Worship*, 1.

7. Schneiders, *Finding the Treasure*, 100.

express the Christian message in the concepts and language of different peoples . . . it was an attempt to adapt the gospel to the understanding of all."[8] These concepts and language are what make up the culture of a particular people. In their research, Gibbs and Bolger found that "historically, discerning missionaries have engaged the culture, seeking to communicate the gospel in indigenous forms while remaining faithful to Scripture."[9] The Church has always addressed its message in terms that particular groups of people can understand. As seen above, youth are a group of people bound by the problems of development and age that bonds them together in a shared identity. Therefore, the Church is called to speak to youth.

Taking into account all that has been discussed thus far, we can state our thesis: the Church is called to adapt the Gospel to culture; youth is a culture; the Church must understand, work with, and adapt the Gospel to youth culture to minister effectively with youth. We communicate the Gospel to particular cultures, but we also remain "faithful to Scripture."[10] In the Catholic Church, we adapt the Gospel to this particular culture of youth while remaining faithful to the Scriptures, our Tradition of continuing the faith of the apostles, the Magisterium, which is the teaching body of the church and its teachings, and the continued, Spirit-led life of the Church as we know it and live it. It is a careful line to be walked, but with a fuller understanding of this particular culture and an open mind, we can present the gospel message faithfully to the next generation.

8. Flannery, *Vatican Council II*, 946.

9. Gibbs and Bolger, *Emerging Churches*, 17.

10. Ibid.

This book is an exploration of the characteristics of contemporary youth and some practical strategies that will enable effective ministry with this culture. The focus will be particularly on the ministry challenges brought about by postmodernism. The common thread throughout this study will be that contemporary youth culture can best be seen as part of the larger concept of postmodern culture. Our study will begin by defining the characteristics of the historic eras of modernity and postmodernity. We will apply these findings to youth and paint a picture of what today's postmodern youth look like. After looking at a brief history of youth ministry in the past century and a quick examination of some failed attempts to work with this culture, we will come finally to some key elements of a postmodern youth ministry. We begin our study with an overview of the Modern Age.

Modernism

THE LIST of labels that can be applied to historic epochs is seemingly endless. The first major division
that can be agreed upon, though with no definite date, is
that between history and prehistory. Prehistory is that time
before written records.[1] Before we come to the Modern
Age, we have the Premodern Age. Premodern is different
from prehistory. There are many more subdivisions that we
could include within Premodern: Ancient, Late Ancient,
Dark Ages, Early Medieval, High Medieval, Late Medieval,
Renaissance, Early Modern, etc. Not all of these strictly follow premodern characteristics, but the key characteristics
of this age were still present throughout. "Premodern human beings believed that the universe was the playground
of the gods or God. Life was beyond human control and
could be explained only in supernatural terms. Natural
disasters and illness were interpreted as signs of divine dis-
pleasure. Chaos reigned in the universe. The only way to
bring order to human existence was to befriend or placate
the gods, thus ensuring their cooperation in battling the
evil and the chaos."[2] Fear, sacrifice, and supplication rule

1. Segal, "Western Civ," 774.
2. Nash, *An 8-Track Church*, 13–14.

throughout this age, which includes the religions of early humanity; i.e. Egyptians, Greeks, Romans, Judaism, and Christianity. "The church existed within this premodern worldview through its first seventeen centuries. The early church was born into a pluralistic context in which various religions sought to explain reality and to offer hope and solace to their constituents . . . the idea of God's absolute power and authority over all of human life formed the foundation for the premodern Christian worldview."[3] Even into the Reformation, premodernism remained, but the seeds were planted for change.

The definite time of the Modern Age comes with Rene Descartes in 1641 with the publication of *Meditations on First Philosophy*, which includes his *cogito*: "I think, therefore, I am." Descartes' goal was to find the truths of existence without being prejudiced by any mistakes made by previous philosophers throughout history. He began by doubting all that he saw and experienced around him. One by one he eliminated the people and things in the world around him. He proceeded with this until he doubted all that existed, even God. What he was left with was the insight that even within this realm of doubt of all that is, he himself still was present as the one thinking these thoughts.[4] He then proceeded to rebuild an entire system of philosophy and explanation of all that is from this foundation. What made this so revolutionary was the fact that the base of his thought is the human being as a rational creature. The existence of everything, including God, was derived from the existence of one person. With this placement of the human at the center of

3. Ibid., 14.

4. Descartes, *Meditations on First Philosophy*, 17–24.

attention, and the center of the universe, the world moved away from the medieval and premodern mindset of God at the center.

With the *cogito* as our starting point, we can proceed to a summary of the entire Modern Age. As Matt Kelley states, "the human mind is lifted up as the apex of evolution because of its capacity to reason."[5] We have moved through the ages of the premodern, with mystery and crediting all things to a distant God, to a time of the fullness of evolution where the human mind alone can comprehend all the secrets of the universe through the use of reason. "From this anthropocentric self-understanding which so characterizes modernity come all the features of modernity."[6]

As we have seen, the *cogito* does not just make humanity the center. The wording actually places the "I," the personal subject, at the center of attention. Everything other than the "I" was pushed aside, as all of reality and the truths of existence were found within myself. Descartes made "I" the center and everything else was "Other." It is "I" alone that can answer all of the questions, with only the help of my own reason. Reason and logic examine the world and discover certain similarities, consistencies, and commonalities. These similarities are studied and theories, axioms, and laws are developed to explain everything, which can then be used to explain new situations by applying these laws. The modern mind looks at what unites things and what is recognizable in new things. Gibbs and Bolger's exploration found that "inherent to the logic of modernity was a resolve to remove the ambivalent, to remove all that

5. Kelley, "An Introduction to Postmodernism," para. 5.

6. Schneiders, *Finding the Treasure*, 111.

did not fit."[7] What unites us is what is true. Everything that makes us different or unique is ignored or left to accident and unimportant.[8]

With this emphasis on reason, what of the mystical or the idea of faith? Reason can solve everything; as it tosses out all that is unreasonable, it downplays faith. All the miracles and the fantastic stories of the saints and the Bible are removed from consideration as they cannot be explained by reason. Religion itself is scrutinized under the objective lens of reason. Taking into consideration the concept of the "Other," the objects that are beyond myself need to be analyzed, but in doing this, the process creates a self-centeredness. I am always the one analyzing, with the beginning of each phase of the process seen in terms of my own experience. Each analysis treats anything beyond myself as something to be observed and compared to myself. All thought of anything other than myself still involves myself. If I can comprehend all things with my own reason alone, I do not need other people. "All connections with others became 'extra' and discretionary rather than understood as essential to being human."[9]

This creates now a lack of need for other people, which can be seen most clearly in the realm of religion. The wisdom of scripture reaffirms the theological position that God created humanity as a community. When Adam was alone in the garden, God provided companionship and community. "It is not good for the man to be alone." (Gen 2:18) In the "Dogmatic Constitution on the Church" from the Second

---

7. Gibbs and Bolger, *Emerging Churches*, 118.

8. Carson, *Transforming Worship*, 23.

9. Gibbs and Bolger, *Emerging Churches*, 92.

Vatican Council, we are taught that God has "willed to make men holy and save them, not as individuals without any bond or link between them, but rather to make them into a people."[10] We need community. To believe otherwise is dangerous for Christians, and all of humanity. It can lead to isolationism, a belief that humanity can do everything by itself. This is not true in terms of looking at all of the services we enjoy every day that others help provide, but in terms of denying the need for church or a faith community. The modern mindset believes that we can survive quite well now alone. We do not need God anymore. Our reason is enough to provide all of the answers.

All systems were questioned and reevaluated after the Enlightenment. The great system of humanity's relationship with the divine and the supernatural were brought under the eye of scrutiny. Modernism believed that humans can survive on their own. Reason and its child, science, explained everything that used to be credited to or "blamed" on a god. Religion itself was measured by its reasonableness, not its efficacy. "Rationality is the measure of all truth, and reason is the chief means to knowledge."[11] The revelation that is taught by the Church has been put aside so that humanity can find the truth through its own process of doubt and investigation. "Traditional structures of authority (like the church) were challenged because they were considered to be an affront to people's ability to think and reason for themselves."[12]

10. Flannery, *Vatican Council II*, 359.

11. Carson, *Transforming Worship*, 23.

12. Kelley, "An Introduction to Postmodernism," para. 6.

With the loss of the traditional structures comes the loss of tradition itself. Anything that hinted at the supernatural, the mystical, or the magical was removed from sight. We were left with what was knowable, reasonable, and provable; with what could be seen, touched, and felt. This was considered to be the "Truth." Truth and its smaller components, truths, can be applied as laws to all aspects of life. The world, as seen through the eyes of reason, follows certain truths. Robert J. Nash, a self-proclaimed postmodern character educator, claims that, "moral absolutists believe Background Truths that are presumed to be free from variability and error, that are underived, complete, and universally binding."[13] Only that which can be proved conclusively is true and these truths can then be applied to future discoveries and questions. As stated earlier, the Modern Era is characterized by a search for what unites humanity. This search is the ultimate search for truth and a fuller explanation of the world. Any evidence that leads away from this unity is thrown out. "Nonrational knowing is always subservient to rational knowing, or else it is discounted entirely. Things we can't prove or understand don't really exist."[14]

What are the ramifications then for all of the other concepts, evidences, and observations that do not fit neatly into the laws, the systems, or the universal truths that reason shows? Philosophers form theories based on evidence gained through reason in the search for truth. Truth is gained by being able to "prove" something is so, much as in geometry and logic a "proof" is used to guide theories step

13. Nash, "A Postmodern Reflection," 255.

14. Carson, *Transforming Worship*, 23.

by step to a conclusion: the answer. Even though in reality it may be seen and touched physically, it is not "real" for philosophy unless it can be proven. Philosophy itself would even ask the question "What is 'real'?"

While being cast out of the mind of the philosopher, however, the minority views from the Modern Age do indeed still exist. While the majority view writes history, minorities continue to survive. Yet they are forced to remain "minor." Opinions that are not a part of that majority are downplayed and ignored. The people and groups that hold these ideas or are the minority themselves are taken out of consideration as an influential force in the destiny of history. An emphasis is placed on fitting in with the majority, on conforming to the dominant view. Keeping in mind that history is written by the winners, the winners of our Modern Age can be seen in who is promoted in the majority view. It can be seen in the ethnocentrism of the white, male, Western elite. All others are minorities. Yet this majority should not be confused with an actual like-minded community. It is not an actual sharing of life, just a sharing of space.

Postmodernism

WITH THESE characteristics of modernity in place, we can turn our attention to the historic situation in which we now find ourselves. The Modern Era lasted from "roughly the 1500s to about the 1960s (and, of course, it is still the dominant worldview)."[1] Throughout this discussion of the Modern Age, the premise being followed is that postmodernism is not actually an era or historic epoch in and of itself. It is a reaction against modernism. The specific meanings of these statements will be explicated throughout this section.

The best way to explain this reaction is through an understanding of "Hegelian historicism."[2] Georg Hegel presents the concept of the *dialectic* in *Phenomenology of the Spirit* (1806).

> The truth was revealed through a process of successive contradictions by which an initial proposition, a *thesis* if you will, is shown to be in-adequate for explaining some phenomenon and, therefore, another proposition (perhaps an op-posite) emerges to challenge its place. This might be called an *antithesis*. They run side by side,

1. Schneiders, *Finding the Treasure*, 111.
2. Rorty, "The Continuity," 20.

challenging each other. Soon, however, this new proposition proves to be weak or inadequate and so the best elements of each—the most rational elements—form a *synthesis*. This process of consolidation is referred to as *sublimation* wherein the weaker elements are absorbed or consumed into the stronger thesis. This new synthesis becomes a new thesis and this triadic system repeats itself through time until an ultimate total, comprehensive truth is arrived at. What he refers to as Absolute Truth is but a collection of all possible triads in the universe.[3]

No one thought or system of thoughts is the final word. There will always come along a new way of looking at things, until we come to the final, Absolute Truth; which is a summary of all these phases that led to it, as all syntheses contain elements from all previous theses and antitheses. The modern worldview will have something to challenge it one day. The synthesis is not automatic, though. The thesis and antithesis continue together for a time. The synthesis is achieved when the best of its base elements are understood and the weaker elements are cast aside. An ongoing premise for our study is that modernity is the thesis, postmodernity is but the antithesis, and we still await the synthesis of what will be.

Closer to our own time, "what happened during the very late nineteenth and early twentieth centuries, scholars agreed, was a revolt against the positivism, rationalism, realism, and liberalism that the Victorian intellectuals had

3. Solerno, *Beyond the Enlightenment*, 12.

refined from the Enlightenment."[4] This revolt contained the seeds of the new antithesis of postmodernism. In hindsight we have the academic Hegelian Dialectic as a model to guide us through this process now, but the beginnings of postmodernism are actually outside the purely academic. For example, the United States stock market crash of 1929 "and the ensuing Great Depression displayed the limits of humanity's ingenuity and will to succeed."[5] The great success of humanity's ability to use reason to solve all problems came up against the reality of breadlines, poverty, and the insecurity of life. People began to ask questions and tried to discover what went wrong.

"Postmodernism," as a term, according to Tyron Inbody, "originated in art (specifically architecture) and literature . . . since the 1940s or 1950s."[6] Postmodern opposes modernity's order and right angles in terms of form; with its asymmetry, curves, harsh angles, and overall sense of disorder.[7] Within literature, poetry showed best a lack of form, even down to printing techniques, with words in random places on a page or lines running circularly around the page. A perfect example comes from this book's bibliography in Tony Jones' book *Postmodern Youth Ministry*. This book's whole layout is postmodern: with changing fonts and sizes, blurred text, and slanting lines.[8]

4. Hollinger, "The Enlightenment," 11.

5. Kelley, "An Introduction to Postmodernism," para. 8.

6. Inbody, "Postmodernism," 523.

7. Examples include the Guggenheim Museum in Bilbao, Spain; the Seattle Public Library; and the Peter B. Lewis Building at Case Western Reserve University in Cleveland, Ohio.

8. Jones, *Postmodern Youth Ministry*.

These attempts to break free of the bonds and rules of modernism emerged in thought and philosophy clearly in the aftermath of World War II. The Holocaust signaled the necessity of a new worldview. The murder of millions, the attempted extermination of an entire people, and the seeming blind-eye of those who should have known about it; all color our view of what humanity is capable of and what can be done in the name of progress. "Many have come to see . . . mass death events as outcomes of characteristically modern developments in science and technology, political, sexual, social and economic organization, and forms of 'progress.'"[9] The resulting theories are not really new ways of thinking. They are just ways of reacting against the old ways of thinking that no longer appear to work.

"Postmodernity is primarily characterized by the loss of the unitary worldview and the resulting fragmentation of reality on every level."[10] A good way to illustrate this point is to go back to the origins of postmodernity in literature. All of the individual characters and scenes are tied together by the plot. In postmodernity, a plot is no longer necessary. The character can develop independently and scenes can occur in any order. Once we get into postmodernism as a worldview, this point is developed into the idea that there really is no plot unifying the story of existence. In philosophy, this unifying plot is what Schneiders is calling the unitary worldview. More broadly in terms of this study, what makes this view united is the metanarrative. "A *metanarrative* is a master story that one believes comprehends the

---

9. Inbody, "Postmodernism," 528.
10. Schneiders, *Finding the Treasure*, 112.

whole of reality and into which one's own story fits."[11] The metanarrative was what reason had discovered was the underlying truth. It was the way in which commonality could be explained and future events could be predicted. In the Judeo-Christian story, Salvation History is a metanarrative. Our journey of faith from our origins as the Hebrew people called by God, through the revelation of Jesus Christ, and continuing now in the life of the Church, is one long metanarrative. It is a way for Christians to tell their story and to share a belief system and a bond. Postmodernity's critique of the metanarrative is that it only speaks to the common, majority experience. What of the experiences of the minority? Chuck Smith resolves this in that, "postmodernity calls our attention to the many, varied, and local narratives of each culture or group."[12] Instead of modernity's push to see what we have in common and oppression of all that is "Other," the voice of the minority is brought back to our attention. The positive aspects of this are that those who did not have a voice, now do. A metanarrative can no longer be used to oppress or push down another. All metanarratives are brought into question. The end result though is that all metanarratives are denied any truth. Postmodernists do not believe that metanarratives even exist. With no underlying worldview, all thought and belief becomes the local narratives of each culture and ultimately each individual, returning us back to the beginnings of the Modern Age and Descartes' original subject "I." The subjective triumph of reason in the Modern Age has surpassed

11. Ibid., 113.

12. Smith, *The End of World*, 51.

any need for objectivity. There is no longer any basis for objective truth; everything is subjective.

"A variety of postmodernist philosophies and postmodern social conditions have tended to undermine the notions that objective truth exists in the first place."[13] With no objective truth, how can there be any truth at all? How can we speak of truth without appealing to an exterior, underlying doctrine or code? To answer this we again examine the character educational system of Nash. Within his teaching, he uses phrases like "morals" and "virtues" quite often. Yet he is quick to point out that the morals and virtues that each of us hold are just as important as anyone else's and must be taken into account. For Nash, truth is obtained through dialogue. His formation in character education is only successful "whenever it emerges from an honest exchange of opposing points of view in a free and open encounter."[14] Different cultures and peoples would sit down together and talk about what they believe. The end result would be a consensus of what they believed was real and what the truth was. If the result is useful to some of the individuals, they will incorporate them into their own lives. If the resulting consensus was not acceptable to other individuals, they may disregard it and continue as they were.[15] Using Jones' book again as an example; in the writing of the book, Jones invited colleagues to provide commentary and critique to his ideas. These comments, positive and negative, are included throughout the text. This allows Jones to illustrate the point that it is not just his point of view that is

13. Groothuis, "Why Truth Matters," 47.

14. Nash, "A Postmodern Reflection," 246.

15. Ibid., 256.

valid; other opinions are available on the same page for the reader to judge her own truth.[16]

While Nash feels quite happy with this process, elsewhere Joseph F. Rychlak presents a different point of view that illustrates the faults with a dialogue that Nash propounds. Without any way to enforce a final answer, without any underlying or connecting story to appeal, and without common language to use for definitions; "we are locked into an unsolvable exchange of dialogue, discussing all sides of conflicting issues without hope of achieving even a relative, arbitrary, culture-bound truth."[17] Nash's conversations would be eternal sharing with no results.

Remembering again the tenets of the Modern Age, the majority view became the truth. Metanarratives were seen as tools of oppression and injustice at the cost of minorities. The majority controlled the truth. So now within postmodernity, as David Couchman helps us to see, "people suspect truth claims, not only because they think it isn't possible to know the truth, but because they see the claim itself as an attempt to exert power over the lives of other."[18] Claims of objective truth have always been made by the modernists in power and so the minority voice of postmodernity rejects all claims to a single truth. There is a truth for each view. What may be true in my own life could not hold true for another's experience. A postmodernist would claim that I must acknowledge that this is only my truth and that I must respect others' truths. Yet even creating this appeals to a metanarrative of respect for each other that maybe my own

16. Jones, *Postmodern Youth Ministry*.

17. Rychlak, *The Human Image*, 38.

18. Couchman, "Understanding the Times," 48.

truth does not recognize. If I believe as truth that I do not have to respect what anyone else believes, how can anyone tell me to believe otherwise?

With all of these competing truths, dialogues, and opinions; a certain amount of questions and paradoxes arise over the very reality we see around us. Yet this question also shows the continued influence of modernism. What does it matter to a postmodernist what real is? A postmodernist can live with the paradoxes; they can hold two disparate concepts in their minds at the same time and not see a problem. "Reality is just the never-ending, frenetic dance of finite, relative, momentarily connected scraps of existence."[19] All experiences are purely subjective occurrences. The only connection between them is the fact that I am the one experiencing them. The only real reality is my own.

Problems with this extreme view can be illustrated once again in the realm of literature, specifically by viewing the Bible as literature. A believer would appeal to the Bible as the record of Salvation History and the Word of God. A non-believing postmodernist would not recognize any objective truth within the text. "A critical approach to Scripture . . . raised the question of the reliability and verifiability of the events narrated therein. No single worldview can claim preeminence over all others for rationality is traditioned . . . in light, therefore, of both the historical difficulties associated with the resurrection, and the *traditioned* nature of rationality, how can the Christian tradition claim with any warrant, an authoritative and normative revelation?"[20] "Traditioned" here meaning that

19. Schneiders, *Finding the Treasure*, 112.

20. O'Neil, "Ethics and Epistemology," 33.

the text meant one thing at a certain time and history, but that through time and circumstances of editing and understanding, there are many interpretations of what it could mean now. There is a loss of cohesion within the text itself as well. One could not simply say that the Bible is "true," either in a fundamentalist or a moralist manner. Now, O'Neil's purpose is not to assert "that the New Testament documents are basically unreliable, but to acknowledge the impossibility of certifiable knowledge."[21] The doctrines and beliefs of any faith could not be transmitted by simply saying they are true. The truths of faith and belief cannot be reasoned out with a pure postmodernist. Established religions themselves are in danger in the postmodern world from this view, but all is not lost.

While a postmodernist might bristle at being called religious, most claim to be spiritual. "To the postmodern mind, spirituality is not the same as religion. Religion speaks of rigidity, structure, and institutionalism; whereas spirituality is about personal growth and wholeness."[22] Whatever spiritual practice leads to my personal growth, I will choose it and make it my own. And as paradoxes are not a problem, I can choose from many different religious, philosophical, and spiritual practices.[23] It is at this point that organized religion makes an impact on postmodernism. An example comes from the idea of the *Emerging Church* in the writings of Gibbs and Bolger. "Popularly, the term *emerging church* has been applied to high-profile, youth-oriented congregations that have gained attention on account of

21. Ibid., 35.

22. Couchman, "Understanding the Times," 38.

23. Ibid., 51.

their rapid numerical growth; their ability to attract (or retain) twentysomethings; their contemporary worship, which draws from popular music styles; and their ability to promote themselves to the Christian subculture through websites and by word of mouth."[24] The *Emerging Church* described by Gibbs and Bolger points to the sociological insights that today's young adults respond better to "new forms of churches" that "have restored an atmosphere of mystery and awe enhanced by the use of incense, candles, and prayer rituals."[25] While denying the truth of Tradition, these churches are embracing the traditions of the high churches' ceremonials. The stark realism and whitewashed functionalism of the previous generation's churches revealed that "when the mystery, the visual, the ritual, the touch, and the beauty are removed, little is left."[26] After this desert of reason, postmodernists hunger for the mystical and the other-worldly. It is not about making sense; it is about using our senses. It is not about appealing to the mind; it is about feeling and experiencing something beyond ourselves. The world of technology and the self-defeating hallmarks of modernist subjectivism have led to a hunger for something outside my own head; a possible reality that is "Other." They search for what was lost in the Age of Reason, "therefore, the postmodern connection with the ancient can be naturally strong," as Timothy Carson found in his study on *Transforming Worship*. "This means that ancient symbol, ritual, processions, sensory aids, smells, bells, and candles

24. Gibbs and Bolger, *Emerging Churches*, 41.

25. Ibid., 21.

26. Ibid.

all bridge easily into postmodern consciousness."[27] The new antithesis of postmodernism includes aspects of the previous thesis of the *pre*modern, which were synthesized into modernism. So also will aspects of the thesis of modernism be synthesized with the antithesis of postmodernism in the new synthesis.[28]

Yet this is not a total disconnect from contemporary technology. While postmoderns reclaim the mystical, they still have the technological resources of the world at hand. A good example of this paradox can be seen in the Eternal Word Television Network. Schneiders claims that Mother Angelica and EWTN use "postmodern technology to promote a premodern form."[29] The ancient prayer of the rosary can be seen by millions and the very rosaries can then be ordered on the Internet. Yet we must be on our guard when speaking of the technological world of the postmodern. "The last decade has seen the rise of the Internet, cell phones, and other communication technologies that were supposed to bring us all closer together. Instead they have isolated us from actual human contact. Postmodernism . . . rejects the false claims that technology will bring us together."[30] Many experience depression after hours, even months, of online chatting. Nothing can replace actual community with another living, breathing human. The mistakes of the modernist self-sufficiency and consumer-community are happily being challenged by the lessons learned by the postmodernists.

27. Carson, *Transforming Worship*, 28.

28. We will return to this rediscovery of ritual in Chapter 5.

29. Schneiders, *Finding the Treasure*, 116.

30. Kelley, "An Introduction to Postmodernism," para. 19.

It is not only in terms of emotional development that the necessity of community is seen. "Knowing that one cannot understand all truth on their own, that other cultures might inform my worldview, and that no one can have the market cornered on truth causes the postmodern person to seek community."[31] With so many different aspects of truth raised by the differing minority voices and cultures and so many new and accelerating concepts and technologies, we need each other to keep up a certain knowledge base. We need each other to continue Nash's truth consensus. We simply need each other.

The list of subtypes of postmodernism grows beyond the rational, as Inbody lists: "cultural postmodernism, liberationist postmodernism, deconstructive postmodernism, constructive postmodernism, mystical postmodernism, eschatological postmodernism, reactionary postmodernism,"[32] No matter in what category we may find ourselves, the fact of the matter is that we are in a different age. Whether we believe postmodernism to be the new historic epoch, or that it is simply the twilight of the Modern Age; it is a different world. We are in the midst of a new antithesis. The changes that began in art, politics, philosophy, religion, and technology since the 1930s through the 1960s have forever transformed our worldview.[33]

31. Wood, "Congregationalism," 68.

32. Inbody, "Postmodernism," 523–37.

33. Further reading in the sources of postmodern philosophy includes the following classics: Jacques Derrida, *Of Grammatology*, 1976; Michael Foucault, *The Order of Things*, 1966 and *The Archaeology of Knowledge*, 1969; and Jean-Francois Lyotard, *The Postmodern Condition: A Report on Knowledge*, 1979, which coined the phrase "grand narrative."

So we ask along with the late Pope John Paul II: "On what foundations must we build the new historical era that is emerging from the great transformations of the twentieth century? Is it enough to rely on the technological revolution now taking place, which seems to respond only to criteria of productivity and efficiency, without reference to the individual's spiritual dimension or to any universally shared ethic values?"[34]

34. John Paul II, "Evening Vigil," §2.

3

Postmodern Youth

A S WE wait for whatever synthesis or epoch is next to
come; ministers must still look at the present reality in
which they find themselves. The call to preach the Gospel
is coupled with the need to adapt this Gospel to particular
cultures. Decisions must be made as to how to deal with the
characteristics of this postmodern culture and the world in
which they, and many of us, live. For those in youth and
young adult ministry, the culture being worked with is the
postmodern culture, as pointed out by Matt Kelley: "Those
who are truly interested in ministering to youth today have
to understand and engage postmodernism, because whether
we recognize it or not this generation is highly influenced
by postmodern attitudes."[1] So our examination now turns
to explore specifics about the postmodern youth.

As an overview to begin, Roland Martinson, in his
2002 article "Spiritual But Not Religious: Reaching an
Invisible Generation," delves into the general characteristics
that he has discovered about the "Millennial Generation"
(born 1982–present):

---

1. Kelley, "An Introduction to Postmodernism," para. 2.

- 40 percent grew up as latchkey kid, raised self
- See a great chasm between the language, the symbols, and the music of the church and the realities of their world.
- Serious about life
- Convinced that the quality of life is at stake in their decisions
- Stressed out
- Self-reliant
- Skeptical
- Spiritual (mystical, diverse, and often syncretistic), but few interested in Religion
- Spirituality shaped by pop culture
- Know little of major faith traditions
- Survivors
- Realistic rather than idealistic
- No common metanarrative that gives coherence to a universal world
- Experience is their prime referent regarding truth 'If we've experienced it, we know it to be true.'
- Either relativists or fundamentalists[2]

Taking all of these as a starting point, we will explore in greater depth some of the key characteristics. Specifically, the portrait of the postmodern youth should become visible by coloring in the concepts of the lack of metanarrative,

2. Martinson, "Spiritual But Not Religious," data throughout article.

the lack of objective truth, experience as the prime refer-ent, the saying "spiritual, but not religious," and the need for community. Harold Horell summarizes the situation: "Generally, contact among ethnic groups within denomina-tions, life situations that create connections across Christian denominations or between Christians and people of other faiths, the realities of single-parent and blended families, and a host of other postmodern complexities create situa-tions in which established structures of meaning and value no longer prove to be adequate."[3]

It begins by breaking down a barrier between "us" and "them," actually talking to each other. The world is getting smaller with technological advances. With this increased sharing of experiences and cultures, more and more groups are uncomfortable with damning each other outright. We reevaluate the theological implications of the statement that there is "no salvation outside the church." More and more attention is placed on what we have in common, yet also beginning to appreciate what makes us different and unique. Metanarratives were built up as stories that could explain it all. Reason could cover all the possibilities. Yet after two world wars, the Depression, and the Holocaust; we are left picking up the crumbling pieces of the story; trying to make sense over how this could have happened. The metanarratives in place did not save us and do not ex-plain how these came about. All confidence that the same metanarratives will be able to protect in the future is gone. "The question for today's youth is whether they can find a story large enough to challenge the systemic brokenness of

3. Horell, "Fostering Hope," 23.

the world."[4] Since we are already looking at those harmed by the metanarratives of the past, we continue to look at them and listen to their own individual stories. The individual stories of each culture have a truth and a life of themselves. Perhaps a grand, unifying theory of the world is no longer needed, as attempts to do so in the past failed.

The metanarrative gave cohesion to the disjointed events of our lives. It was a way to ground us in a common language to explain reality. Without the commonality, there are only individual occurrences, and without the explanation, reality loses its real-ness. "Reality is a text open to myriad interpretations, and meaning is constructed by the self and subject to constant change."[5] Reality and meaning only exist as far as we allow them to exist. This gives a great sense of power, along with a great sense of fear, to our youth today, "in light of postmodernism's dismissal of metanarratives and its readiness to label any strongly argued convictions as dogmatism, intellectual imperialism, and the like. While one cannot reduce the concept of truth to power relationships . . . truth and falsity is partially determined by those who control the discourse."[6] Our postmodern youth are used to discussing world views with those of other cultures or reading about them on the internet. With so much information available at once, our youth can become overwhelmed. Each piece of information must somehow be accepted. Any form of evaluation would mean holding it up to a system or theory to test whether we believe it or not. Such systems and theories are metanarratives, which have

4. White, "Illusions," 20.

5. Engebretson, "Young People," 17.

6. Groothuis, "Why Truth Matters," 53.

been denied to this generation. So any connections between the avalanche of information are impossible.

All metanarratives are denied, including that of Salvation History. The story of the Chosen People, the mission of Jesus, and the life of the Church are all part of one long metanarrative. Included in the two Testaments are stories that explain every aspect of humanity's relationship with God and path towards salvation. Yet gone are the days of triumphant Church history. Our children are aware of scandalous popes, glutinous monks, greedy friars, and other less proud moments in the Church. As with many other organizations, the Church as well did not have the answers the world needed in the early part of the twentieth century. The Catholic Church suffered in the first half of the last century and it was sixty years before the Church could begin to dialogue with what was happening in the world. It is a new world and our youth distrust the idea that the Church will be able to give them the answers they need. "There is a postmodern sense that we must increasingly face new, unprecedented situations, and that the established truths of Christian worldviews are less and less helpful guides for our lives and faith communities."[7]

Salvation History is our story. It explains our relationship with God and the history of our love affair with our creator. Without a trust in this story, children will be without a guide on their path. Christianity itself has lost its hold as a metanarrative. "We must remember that within postmodernity every subculture and tribe is allowed its own narrative, its own sacred text. Believers can legitimately

7. Horell, "Fostering Hope," 24.

present the Bible to the world as the Christian narrative."[8] Postmodernism only will not let them present it as *the* metanarrative. Even the Bible itself as a guide for life or the deposit of truth is no longer recognized in the postmodern world. It is not a question of whether things in the Bible are true or not; it is a question of what other truths are out there. Even when such teachings may appear to be in conflict with each other, a postmodern can still hold them in tension together. This tension is explained by Kelley: "Postmoderns believe that everything must be questioned . . . they've honestly considered that the alternative might be true."[9] Yet for believers, Salvation History is unique among all other metanarratives. It is not that the revelation of Jesus Christ is one among many stories; the belief "is that there has been given in Jesus of Nazareth a climactic—and not just paradigmatic—revelation of God because of the implications of his resurrection."[10] We believe that Jesus is not just *a* savior, He is *the* savior. How can we pass along this belief in the one true God among so many other competing stories?

A contemporary example would be helpful at this point, from the popular book, *The DaVinci Code*. Among other theories of our Catholic history, author Dan Brown hits at the very core of the texts used in researching Church history, especially the Bible. "The Bible, as we know it today, was collated by the pagan Roman emperor Constantine the Great."[11] Constantine invented the concept of Jesus as a di-

8. Smith, *The End of World*, 189.

9. Kelley, "An Introduction to Postmodernism," para. 14.

10. O'Neil, "Ethics and Epistemology," 33.

11. Brown, *The DaVinci Code*, 231.

vine being at Nicaea in 325 AD. To uphold his claims to the divinity of Christ, Constantine kept writings that show Jesus as divine and omits those that show him as only mortal. The first fallacy here is that in history the opposite is true, especially when we look at the writings that show the *mortality* of Jesus, especially in post-Resurrection accounts,[12] in light of the Docetist heresy that claimed Jesus only "appeared" to be human. The focus for our study is on the collation and authority of the writings in the Bible itself. What was left out by Constantine, according to Brown, were the many Gnostic gospels of the time. Current scholars, such as Bart Ehrman, point out the fact that "it was not until the year 367 C.E., almost two and a half centuries after the last New Testament book was written, that any Christian of record (Athanasius, bishop of Alexandria) named our current twenty-seven books as the authoritative canon of Scripture."[13] It is not until forty years after Nicaea that we see a list of the current books and it is by St. Athanasius. The other judge for authority is the exact nature of how the books were chosen. It was not on the whim of an emperor, but on a practical system that includes three criteria. These three criteria for establishing a writing as 'canon,' according to scripture scholar Raymond Brown, are: "apostolic origin, real or putative," the "importance of the addressed community," and its "conformity with the rule of faith."[14] Dan

12. Cf. Luke 24:43.

13. Ehrman, *A Brief Introduction*, 7.

14. Brown, *An Introduction*, 10–11. Another way to explain the "conformity with the rule of faith" is by the more formal idea of the *sensus fidei*, the sense of the faithful. "The whole body of the faithful . . . cannot err in matters of belief. This characteristic is shown in the supernatural appreciation of faith (*sensus fidei*) on the part of

Brown's book remains just that: a book. It is a good book, but for any serious student of history, there are numerous errors. Yet the papers were filled at the time of its popularity with stories of people leaving the Church or even losing their faith completely. These people believed the book's premise that the creation of the Bible and many of the tenets of the faith that they had been raised with were merely part of an elaborate plot by the Vatican to keep secret the marriage of Mary Magdalene and Jesus; a plot that has been ongoing since the fourth century.[15] Anyone that speaks up for the Church is seen as being part of the conspiracy; another victim of the metanarrative that has led to so much oppression and injustice to women and others for so many years.

Acceptable for postmodern scholars as well is the use of these alternate stories that did not make it into the Bible. This is seen in an article by Richard Rorty: "Thinkers who like to think of themselves as 'postmodern,' and who teach courses in what they call 'cultural studies' often tell stories about non-canonical texts {Gnostic gospels} . . . They do not attempt to weave these together in to a continuous narrative. For they have been taught . . . to be suspicious of metanarratives which try to tie all the texts, canonical and non-canonical, together."[16] Believers, however, would follow the canonical text as they understand it, and dismiss the non-canonicals. But this would be appealing to the

---

the whole people, when, 'from the bishops to the last of the faithful,' they manifest a universal consent in matters of faith and morals." *Catechism*, 34, §92.

15. Brown, *The DaVinci Code*, 254.

16. Rorty, "The Continuity," 24.

metanarrative of the unity of the Bible. So who is to say which version is true?

The best way to show the difference between canonical and non-canonical texts is simply to have the students read some of the stories from the non-canonical texts. I normally use the stories of Jesus' childhood.[17] When upset and bullied, Jesus is seen to smite dead the offender, which has the bully's parents run to complain to Mary and Joseph. Jesus is lectured, leading him to finally relent and raise the dead back to life. The collective "Sense of the Faithful" leads us to not be able to recognize such a Jesus. This just does not fit in with his overall character. Hence this text does not belong in the Bible. Not all of the stories and texts are so easily dispatched, but the teens here begin to see the difference.

Our discussion of the Bible leads us into our next concept of the lack of objective truth. "The Bible does make explicit moral demands, which fly in the face of contemporary thinking."[18] The Bible can only be another narrative to examine, but not a metanarrative. The grand question of postmodernism was given in the Bible itself, when, during the trial of Jesus, Pontius Pilate asked the famous question, "What is Truth?" (John 18:38). We saw earlier that each individual cultural story had a truth. The narrative was true for the tellers. Truth is completely influenced by the truth-holder's experience. The postmodern person, according to Nash, is "less willing to accept . . . that there are unchallengeable moral facts, truths, and virtues that posses a 'real' life

17. Found in the "Infancy Gospel of Thomas." For this and an extensive collection of the non-canonical, or apocryphal, texts, see Roberts, *Ante-Nicene Fathers—Vol. VIII*.

18. Couchman, "Understanding the Times," 49.

of their own, that exist totally separate from personal and social biases."[19] Truth is only viewed as truth because something in life pointed to this experience as true. If another has not yet experienced this same thing, they would not see it as the truth. The postmodern person is content with this paradox. "If you think it's OK then it's OK for you so long as it doesn't hurt anyone else."[20] While this view is positive in terms of human understanding and compassion, it has some negative effects in the realm of morality and ethics. Even if another person believes that what they are doing is OK, we should still step in if we see that what they are doing is actually harmful to themselves. The extreme postmodern view would be that no one can judge the reasons of another and should let them work it out on there own.

Morality is only a personal code. Your ethical beliefs are not binding on anyone other than yourself. Without a metanarrative of "right and wrong," there is nothing to which we can appeal to judge the common good of society or on which to base rules and laws. Postmodern youth fall into a live-and-let-live approach to all points of morality.

Postmodern youth will pay attention and obey the story of one who has "been through it." Experience is the ultimate decider of what is real and true in life. While many drug addicts would tell their story in terms of a plea to convince their audience to not make the same mistakes, the postmodern youth would see the addict as the only authorized expert on the subject of drug use. The experience, no matter how painful, is seen as a positive in that the person has successfully made it through and has lived

19. Nash, "A Postmodern Reflection," 252.
20. Engebretson, "Young People," 12.

to tell the story. This respect for experience is held not just in terms of outside authority, but interior authority as well. "Postmodern teenagers prefer to experience something rather than just hearing about it."[21] The authority that the drug addict spoke with influenced the teen-listener more than the actual message. "For young people experience is central in the search for meaning."[22] They need to experience it as well in order for it to be true for them. The addict speaks with a truth-conviction that inspires, but the truth is not just believed on their word alone. The postmodern youth needs to make it true for them, too. Suffering is a validation of experience and authority. Many will believe that it is actually a good thing that terrible things happen to a person and might actually seek out such terrible things in order to become a stronger person in the future.

The postmodern youth wants to experience everything in order to discover the truth in the world. The Hegelian dialectic showed us that the Absolute will only be attained as a summary of all theses and antitheses. Teens will need to experience everything in order to gain all of the knowledge necessary for the answers. They cannot just take your word for it, as truth is only in the one experiencing it. Without the claims of a single truth in terms of religion either, postmodern youth will want to have as many religious experiences as they can in order to cover all the possible truths of faith. "They are not ideological in that they do not choose one religious system to follow, but they search for meaningful personal experiences that speak to them of the spiritual life."[23]

21. Kelley, "An Introduction to Postmodernism," para. 18.
22. Engebretson, "Young People," 12.
23. Ibid.

Christian faith is described and preached in terms of beliefs and doctrines, but the actual conversion occurs through an experience of Jesus Christ. If this experience is not encouraged in our spiritual formation of young people, they will only have doctrine without a sure foundation. While the result is not necessarily a lack of belief in Christianity or an explicit denial of its teachings, what is present is a lack of commitment to the whole Christian life. Rules can be instilled and followed from one case to the next, but a mature faith grounded in an experience is what will be required. This point is shown by Chuck Smith: "In a postmodern culture, rational arguments against faith no longer carry the same weight. But on the other hand, neither do rational arguments in favor of faith, which means Christians may find their apologetics from the last two centuries to be less and less effective."[24] The faith cannot just be preached without an experiential component. The postmodern youth simply will not be able to see the whole of the faith without an experience of it. It is similar to the movie *The Matrix*. Neo has been searching for years to discover the secret of the Matrix. When he finally finds someone to explain it, he is simply told that he has "to experience it to know it."[25] This helps us see more clearly that it is not the experience alone that imparts knowledge. Neo had already searched and pondered the meaning of the Matrix. The experience finally clarified the knowledge, but was not the whole of it. This can explain how the postmodern youth can still understand and claim belief in the church while holding on to other paradoxical beliefs. Smith tells us that

24. Smith, *The End of World*, 68.
25. Ibid., 85.

"postmodernists . . . want to know by personal experience as well as objective study."[26] Yet this decision in the end is based on the authority of an actual personal experience, not the external knowledge imparted.

All external knowledge is colored by the life experiences of the teacher. The postmodern youth sees the hodge-podge of beliefs that make up their own faith and experience and view the rest of the academic world in a similar way. "Postmoderns recognize that it's almost impossible to be objective about anything. Our socio-economic backgrounds, our upbringings, our friends, our educational levels, and everything else about us influence the way we perceive every situation."[27] The modernist emphasis on the subject, Descartes' "I," continues through postmodernism to the extreme, complete denial of objectivity. Our experiences always color the way we view future experiences. This is true for all other humans as well.

With all of this information gathering and experience attaining, the postmodern youth can fall into the trap of waiting. They can spend their lives waiting for a clearer answer, for *all* the information, and for the grand synthesis of history until making any decisions in life. This procrastination is elucidated by Joseph Rychlak: "Long-standing traditions and loyalties such as entering into formal marriage, specific church membership, or active participation in political parties are not easily adopted."[28] Why rush when everything could be different tomorrow because of a new experience or a new point-of-view? The postmodern youth

26. Ibid.
27. Kelley, "An Introduction to Postmodernism," para. 22.
28. Rychlak, *The Human Image*, 128.

needs to continue to experience as much as they can to the point that the goal becomes the experiences themselves instead of any attainment of knowledge. "Commitments can wait in the eagerness for experience."[29]

The result of all of this searching, experiencing, and lack of commitment is best summed up in the frequently heard saying, "I'm spiritual, but not religious." The postmodern youth recognizes the deep, inner hunger for the mystical and other-worldly that modernism denied, but is unable to commit to the religions that can provide such experiences. They may study religion, but with the denial of objective truth, they would be unable to choose one religion over another as the "right" religion. The truth is only gained through experience, so they would have to experience many different religions in order to discover which one was true. Smith points out the effects of this picking and choosing: "Postmodern religion is eclectic. Believers pick and choose their favorite authors and teachers from among a variety of denominations (and non-denominations) and their theological persuasions. Loyalty to the religious traditions of their parents and grandparents is not important to postmoderns. Since popular culture is no longer strapped by the constraints of neat, rational categories, postmoderns are free to celebrate a new openness to nonrational entities (angels) and experiences (miracles)."[30] This is not what we call "Cafeteria Catholics," who pick and choose which aspects of Catholicism they will follow and those in which they do not believe. Postmodernists are not just picking what they like within the faith. They are picking and choos-

29. Engebretson, "Young People," 18.
30. Smith, *The End of World*, 67.

ing from many different religions and quasi-religions to create their faith. Robert N. Nash points this out by sharing about his experience of finding an overwhelming number of books on angels in a book store. The sales representative told him how popular these books were becoming. He sees it as "a parable of the way Americans have become increasingly interested in issues of spirituality. Books on angels, Eastern religions, meditation, and self-improvement reflect a culture-wide interest in such matters."[31]

Another way to illustrate this point is from the experience of Abbot Thomas Keating. Along with Basil Pennington, their Centering Prayer movement has spread throughout the country and to the world. Keating provides a brief history of Centering Prayer in the introduction to his book *Intimacy with God*. It includes a story of how he became aware of the widespread and "deep contemporary hunger for spirituality."[32] He had lived for many years as a Trappist monk and served as the spiritual head, the abbot, of one monastery, and so was very familiar with the spiritual practices and history of the Catholic Church. After Vatican II, he noticed that many young people were going to India to find a guru to answer the hunger for spirituality. He wondered why more of these young people did not just come to the monasteries in the United States, including his own. He believes that many had no knowledge of the contemplative tradition within Catholicism. So Abbot Keating raised the issue with his own community about outreach and education. "Could we put the Christian tradition into a form that would be accessible to people in the active min-

31. Nash, *An 8-Track Church*, 7.
32. Keating, *Intimacy*, 13.

istry today and to young people who have been instructed in an Eastern technique and might be inspired to return to their Christian roots if they knew there was something similar in the Christian tradition?"[33] The something similar he developed from the Church's history he called Centering Prayer. He held the first such retreat in 1982, which he discovered had a number of fallen-away Catholics. "'Where are these Catholics coming from?' Many of them were disaffected from the religion of their youth because of the legalistic and over moralistic teaching that many had received in their local parishes and Catholic schools; they now felt spiritually enriched by their experiences in Buddhism and Hinduism."[34] The Church they had grown up with, which had not yet even awakened to the Modern Age, let alone the Postmodern, was presented to them as a list of rules and external observances. We can see this still being played out today in our young adults. Once getting through their formative teenage years, as taught by Kathleen Engebreston, they "begin to question the assumption that one can survive without religion. The lack of an integrated religious system has left them hungry for a spirituality."[35] This leads them to the quest for faith, but, as already shown above, the quest does not lead them necessarily to *a* faith.

How much of this situation is the Catholic Church's fault? Could a more open-minded church have been able to hold on to its members throughout the turbulent changes of the sixties? True, the *Catechism of the Catholic Church* today recognizes that "the desire for God is written in the human

33. Ibid., 15.

34. Ibid., 17.

35. Engebretson, "Young People," 13.

heart, because man is created by God and for God; and God never ceases to draw man to himself."[36] Yet was the Church responding and providing a way for this new generation to experience the person of Jesus Christ? Clues are found in the evidence of what happened in the forty-or-so years since the Second Vatican Council, as seen in Schneiders: "Process theology, Latin American liberation theology, feminism, a vastly expanded and deepened biblical culture, Eastern mystical approaches, and a host of psychological perspectives and techniques seemed to offer possible meaningful frames of reference for a personal spirituality emancipated from much of the 'religious baggage' and especially the theological absolutes of preconciliar Catholicism."[37] These absolutes and an emphasis on external observances were not enough to respond to the world-thought changes occurring at that time. Attempts to respond to this generation in other faith traditions and seeds of what the Catholic Church can now do will be discussed below in chapters five and six respectively. For now, we close this discussion of "spiritual, but not religious" with a case study by Harold Horell about one of his postmodern young adults.

> Jerry is not interested in finding a way of bringing together the various strands of his spiritual life into some overarching and comprehensive religious understanding of life. Jerry is content to explore connections between his numerous spiritual practices, note incompatibilities and even inconsistencies among them, and to continue to explore a variety of spiritual paths in

36. *Catechism*, 17, §27.
37. Schneiders, *Finding the Treasure*, 189.

> terms of what 'works for me,' that is, what pro-
> vides him with a sense of centeredness and the
> meaningfulness of life.[38]

As explained in the section above on modernism, God created us to be in community. "It is not good for the man to be alone." (Gen 2:18). This is true as well for our post-modernists. They have recognized this deep need for community. The Modern Age was the time of the suppression of the "Other." The postmodernist recognizes the need for the "Other" and the need to be in union with others. In his "Models for Adolescent Ministry," Arthur Canales shares some statistics from a 1993 survey that bring this need for community to the front of our attention. "The reason that friendships are central to adolescent behavior is due to the fact that family relationships are so unsatisfying:

- 25% of ninth graders spend less than *five minutes* per day with their father;

- 53% of all adolescents spend less than *thirty minutes* per day with their fathers;

- 44% of all adolescents spend less than *thirty minutes* per day with their mothers."[39]

Our youth hunger for community, but are not getting it at home all the time. Even when they do spend time with their families, where is the authority that they also need for their formation? Within many postmodern families, Rychlak sees that "paternal authoritarian rule is avoided if at all possible . . . encourages verbal exchange among the family members, which in turn has everyone evaluating and ex-

---

38. Horell, "Fostering Hope," 25.
39. Canales, "Models," 208.

pressing reasoned preferences."[40] This parenting by family consensus is a hallmark of postmodern thought, as we saw in the writings of Nash earlier.

The postmodern youth will go out and answer this need for community in any way they can find. Whether or not the group is good for them or healthy for them does not always make a difference, as long as they belong to something. Peer pressure is not about forcing someone to do something that they do not want to do; it is about a person going along with the majority without discernment of the morality of the decision, just so they belong. The postmodern youth gravitates towards groups that hold similar interests, but also towards any group that would accept them if necessary. "I associate with people because I choose to, because we have some interest in common. Because I've chosen to be with my group, what they think becomes very important to me, and I'm not likely to go against it."[41] The youth would argue and fight to protect the group that has accepted her, even if she does not believe what they believe. She probably has not even considered the truth of what they believe. It is simply her group and she will stand by them.

As I continue to point out, the Postmodern Age carries over many of the elements of the Modern. One case in particular is the advancement of technology. We live in the age of the internet. We can all speak to anyone anywhere in the world in a second through email. We can find out the news on the other end of the globe instantly. Internet chat rooms have promised community even when you are alone at home. Internet community pages, such as MySpace

40. Rychlak, *The Human Image*, 129.

41. Couchman, "Understanding the Times," 51.

and Facebook, have served as a meeting and sharing space for our young people. Hours of chatting and surfing each evening begin to form the way our students observe reality and relationships. Depression can set in as a cumulative effect of hours of supposed sharing on-line fails to fulfill the need for community. Rob Whitley traces these issues back to our earliest days in America, as seen by Tocqueville in his *Democracy in America*. A prevalent issue he saw in America was the problem of "individualism."[42] We can see the image of the rugged frontiersman that can do it all on his own, pulling himself up by his bootstraps to success. This has led to much of the loneliness and depression in our society. "Individual isolation and diminishing communal networks affect mental health."[43] His study points specifically to internet and on-line gaming use, in that "it could be argued that individualization associated with postmodernity may be considered a risk factor for diverse psychiatric outcomes, including depression, suicide, and anxiety."[44] On-line chatting is not the same as a true friendship with face-to-face conversation or even talking on the phone. With this, and other technological advancements, reality in general can be suspended for the postmodern youth. There is always someone awake on-line to chat with and information pages and games are always available. The rest of the world can take on the same never-ending aspect for our youth as well. "Time is no longer governed, as Genesis proclaimed, by the sun that rules the day and the moon and stars that rule the night. We can have endless days, twenty-four-hour shop-

42. Whitley, "Postmodernity," 353.

43. Ibid., 355.

44. Ibid.

ping or partying in daylight-bright malls or casinos."[45] The party never has to end and the postmodern youth never has to leave his room or face reality to get it.

Bringing to a close this picture of a postmodern youth, it needs to be stated that this is not a complete picture. This has been an examination of the key concepts of postmodernism and how they specifically affect the youth of today. There are many other factors that build a complete picture, such as the basic concepts of adolescent development and the role of sports in the life of youth, but these are outside the scope of this study as they are mainly present in youth in every generation. I have attempted to show the specifics of postmodernism in youth and even this picture is not the complete story for the present generation. Not all students display every, or even any, characteristics of postmodernism. This study was to show the extremes to which postmodernism can affect those to whom we minister and to answer specific questions about the actions and inclinations of our youth. Before we approach some recommendations for how specifically to minister to postmodern youth, we take a moment to reflect on the history and purpose of youth ministry in general.

---

45. Schneiders, *Finding the Treasure*, 114. Cf. Gen 1:16.

4

Youth Ministry

WE BEGIN our study of youth ministry with the beginning of youth. Tim Neufeld provides a possible history, where, "The category of 'adolescence' was not popularized until G. Stanley Hall published a book by that name in 1905."[1] The prevailing theory was that before this point, youth were seen as little adults, still working hard and with few individual rights. Barbara Hanawalt reminds us that Philippe Ariès, along the same lines "in *Centuries of Childhood*, denied that people in the Middle Ages had a concept of childhood and argued that the sentimentalized view of childhood as a special phase of life did not exist until the modern period." Hanawalt then goes on through the next two chapters to refute this thesis, using examples throughout early childhood and adolescent development among peasant families in the Middle Ages.[2] Most youth writings were on apprenticeships and education, especially

1. Neufeld, "Postmodern Models," 195.

2. Hanawalt, *The Ties That Bound*, 171. Cf 171–204. More evidence on medieval times and earlier into late-Classical in Herlihy, "Medieval Children," 109–41. For a more complete study on contemporary adolescent development, the classic is Erikson's *Childhood and Society*, enumerating eight stages of development, with stage 5 being key for our study, with its focus on adolescents ages 13–19.

religious education. In Bainton's study on the Reformation, Erasmus and Martin Luther also added to the concept of religious education particularly for youth. This can be studied in Erasmus' *Colloquies* and the "Small Catechism" of Luther in 1529, intended for children. The catechisms were preceded by "five volumes of religious booklets for children . . . produced by his assistants for use in church and school."[3] These examples show an emphasis on youth religious education, but are still not focused ministry for youth.

Churches began to treat children separately and particularly as a result of the postmodern emphasis on minority and the "Other," but this ministry was not true youth ministry as we would see it today. "Through the 1960s virtually the only model of church youth ministry involved parents and adults operating as sponsors and/or teachers for their youth."[4] The confirmation sponsors, teachers, and parents were entrusted with the care and formation of youth as a way of assisting the pastor in the spiritual care of the whole parish. Outside of the Catholic Church, youth ministry began to enter churches through external groups, such as clubs, summer camps, and sports.

> While parachurch campus ministries such as Youth for Christ (YFC), Young Life (YL), and Fellowship of Christian Athletes (FCA) were founded in the mid-twentieth century, their programs became powerful models for the churches of North America in the 1970s. Many congregations saw the success of these agencies, particularly in the areas of evangelism and fel-

3. Bainton, *The Reformation*, 72–74.
4. Neufeld, "Postmodern Models," 195.

lowship, and began to pattern ministries after them. Many YFC, and YL, and FCA workers took full-time positions in churches, and youth ministry became a serious profession.[5]

These early youth ministers were active Christians who already had a thorough knowledge of youth development and youth needs in the Postmodern Age. Their previous jobs made them ideal to lead the new movement of youth ministry. With time, these future pastors would attend seminaries and be ordained as equal peers with senior pastors. Yet the youth pastor was still seen as a temporary position, a stepping stone towards managing a church. "In the 1990s the model of youth-pastor-as-activities-director began to stagnate and show serious weaknesses."[6] A true youth minister wants to minister to youth and not just bide their time until something better comes along. We will pick this thought up again in Chapter 5 below.

Within the Roman Catholic Church, we step back again to the Modern Age. Many different aspects and practices of modernism and the movement as a whole were condemned by the Catholic Church. One might think that the Church would have been more accepting of modernism because of the good it brought to large systems and organizations with its emphasis on the majority rule and obedience to law. The Church, however, saw the evils in modernism from the beginning, with its emphasis on human reason over God, and the fear that it would lead to using modern study to change the faith. Numerous official condemnations of

5. Ibid.
6. Ibid.

modernism came in the course of a century by the Catholic Church. First was Pope Pius IX, who "turned his back on the modern world and in his *Syllabus of Errors* (1864) denounced those who fondly hoped to reconcile the Church with 'progress and modern civilisation.'"[7] Then modernism was condemned in the encyclical *Pascendi* by Pope St. Pius X on September 9, 1907.[8] The final blow was struck by Pope Pius XII on August 12, 1950, with *Humani Generis*, which attacked and exiled from teaching members of a group that taught *la theologie nouvelle* (the new theology), including M-D Chenu, Henri de Lubac, and Yves Congar.[9]

Change came soon after this final attack. The next Pope, John XXIII, called a Council to examine the Church and its place in the world. In explaining a preliminary meeting leading up to the Council, he explains the great word *aggiornamento* (which means "to bring up to date"): "You've probably heard the word *aggiornamento* repeated so many times. Well, the Holy Church who is ever youthful wants to be in a position to understand the diverse circumstances of life so that she can adapt, correct, improve and be filled with fervor."[10] Then on October 11, 1962, during the opening speech of the Council, Pope John gives us the quote most in line with our present theory of the adaptation of the Gospel: "For the substance of the ancient deposit of faith is one thing, and the way in which it is presented is another."[11] This was a redemption for some of the earlier

7. Hebblethwaite, *Pope John XXIII*, 43.

8. Ibid., 37.

9. Ibid., 228–29.

10. Ibid., 264.

11. Ibid., 432.

silenced theologians, such as Congar in his theory of the "Hierarchy of Truths," where "every truth is expressed in a form which has its own historical conditions."[12] The "Truth" does not change, simply the way in which it is presented, which is the best way to describe our theory of adaptation. As those theologians accused of the heresy of "modernism" were redeemed, their teachings led the way for the actual situation of the "Church in the *Post*modern World." The final irony for these men has came in our own age, with de Lubac and Congar both made Cardinals in the Catholic Church in 1983 and 1994 respectively.

In *Gaudium et Spes*, the "Pastoral Constitution on the Church in the Modern World" from the Second Vatican Council (1962–65), Scheiders sees where, "the council officially recognized what the Church had tried for four hundred years to deny, that the Middle Ages were over and modernity was not only here to stay (they thought) but, properly understood and engaged, could even be seen as part of the divine plan."[13] The Church was finally ready to dialogue with the Modern Age. Schneiders corrects this point in that "as the Council drew back the four-hundred-year-old blackout curtains and threw open the windows of the Church to the fresh air of modernity, what met its startled eyes was not the dewy freshness of a new day dawning but the twilight of a dying age."[14] What a shock to take the enormous step of moving beyond a centuries-old struggle and find that the entire course of history has moved to a new epoch. Yet, as has been shown, the postmodern is not an epoch completely

12. Henn, *The Hierarchy*, 77.

13. Schneiders, *Finding the Treasure*, 103.

14. Ibid.

in its own right, but continues the path of modernism. We can continue to use *Gaudium et Spes* as a guide to map the Church's course through the present reality. We look especially to the opening words: "The joy and hope, the grief and anguish of the men of our time, especially of those who are poor and afflicted in any way, are the joy and hope, the grief and anguish of the followers of Christ as well."[15] The Church cares about this world, this age, and the people within it. What is happening in the world affects the Church. While the Modern Age slowly fades and the Postmodern carries us to whatever comes next, the opening words of the Church's dialogue with today's world still bring comfort and ground our purpose in ministry. Even seen through the evangelical Protestant eyes of Robert N. Nash, after the Second Vatican Council, "Catholicism was freed from some of its captivity to tradition. Its structures were changed to reflect the realities of a new day. Today the Roman Catholic Church is no longer a Western institution. It is arguable the world's most influential religious body. Its vitality is the direct result of its willingness to change its traditions and open itself up to new possibilities in a new day."[16]

For Roman Catholics, Michael Horan states that "youth ministry was born out of the context of religious education efforts following the Second Vatican Council."[17] It begins with the recognition that youth are equal members of the Church. The "Dogmatic Constitution on the Church" (*Lumen Gentium*[18]) from the Second Vatican Council pro-

15. Flannery, *Vatican Council II*, 903.

16. Nash, *An 8-Track Church* , 97.

17. Horan, "Youth Ministry," 30.

18. The theme of the Council is continuously pointed out, as seen

vides the teaching on the equal dignity of all of the baptized. Most, if not all, of the youth with whom we minister
are baptized. "There remains . . . a true equality between
all with regard to the dignity and to the activity which is
common to all the faithful in the building up of the Body of
Christ."[19] A basic guide to forming models for youth ministry was also presented at the Second Vatican Council in
the "Decree on the Apostolate of Lay People." In a subsection on "Young People," the document teaches that "adults
should be anxious to enter into friendly dialogue with the
young, where, despite the difference in age, they could get
to know one another and share with one another their own
personal riches."[20] Adults are being encouraged to inter-
act with young people and here we have a basis for youth
ministry, yet it is still similar to existing models of youth
ministry, with the emphasis on adults already interacting
with youth (teachers, sponsors, parents). The concept of a
special ministry to youth only comes after the Council.

Moving from the Church at the international level,
we can focus on the history and writings of the Catholic
Church in America in particular. In 1977, the United States
Conference of Catholic Bishops (U.S.C.C.B.) first addressed
the new approach to youth ministry in its publication *A
Vision of Youth Ministry*.[21] This document provided a basic
framework for youth ministers on how to care for youth

---

in the title of this document, translated as "Light of the Nations." The
Church is the beacon of light, the city on a hill (Matt 5:14), casting
Christ's light and hope to the world.

19. Flannery, *Vatican Council II*, 389.

20. Ibid., 780.

21. U.S. Bishops, *Renewing the Vision*, 4.

within the Church, assist in planning programs, and efficiently run a youth group. The document helped, but little is heard of it today. "For decades youth ministry has been patterned after, and comfortable with, one or two basic models of operation, but with the onset of the postmodern culture, those models are no longer valid."[22] The bishops of the United States returned to the topic of youth ministry themselves and published *Renewing the Vision: A Framework for Youth Ministry* in 1997. The basic purpose was to update the twenty-year-old *Vision of Youth Ministry* and to present a new framework for youth ministry within each diocese and parish. It takes into account Neufeld's point above on the limited efficacy of using a single model of youth ministry. "Ministry with adolescents will need to be more comprehensive and community-wide to take full advantage of the opportunities presented by this research."[23] Instead of relying on one youth minister to "play with the kids," the youth minister becomes a coordinator of youth ministries in partnership with all other ministries in the parish. "The comprehensive approach uses *all* of our resources as a faith community—people, ministries, programs—in a common effort."[24] It takes into account *Gaudium et Spes*' teaching on the equal dignity of all the baptized and treats the youth as equal members of the parish community. The comprehensive approach, according to *Renewing the Vision*, revolves around eight key components to working with youth. "Ministry with adolescents utilizes each of the Church's ministries—advocacy, catechesis, community life,

22. Neufeld, "Postmodern Models," 194.

23. U.S. Bishops, *Renewing the Vision*, 7.

24. Ibid., 19–20.

evangelization, justice and service, leadership development, pastoral care, prayer and worship—in an integrated approach. Each ministry component supports and enhances the others. A comprehensive ministry with adolescents provides balance among all eight components."[25] The comprehensive youth ministry framework allows for the demands of postmodernism as well. Youth are involved in the parish and accepted as they are. Comprehensive youth ministry does care for the communal needs of youth, but does not demand participation in a "youth group" as the only opportunity for community. Some of our kids do not like some of the other kids. Some of them do not have time to meet in a group at the same time as others. A comprehensive approach allows for the pastoral care and involvement of *all* youth in the parish. By not relying solely on a youth group, the youth minister is able to care for a broader population of youth, while still providing experiences for his more active members. The youth minister is then able to carry youth over the bridge of adolescence along with the Church, instead of without it. The necessity of an effective, comprehensive youth ministry program in every parish cannot be overestimated. "Adolescents who participate in parish young ministry programs identify faith and moral formation as a significant contribution to their life, have a profound sense of commitment to the Catholic Church, attend Sunday Mass regularly, and show continued growth while they remain involved in youth programs."[26] Youth Ministry is the prime way to care for the youth in the life of the Church and help them to live fully as Christians. The

25. Ibid., 26.

26. Ibid., 5.

Christian life can be lived fully already within the parish because of youth ministry. Adolescence is not a phase to be endured until adulthood, it is a time to be embraced and celebrated. As Pope John Paul II declared at the World Youth Day in Toronto: "Do not wait until you are older in order to set out on the path of holiness! Holiness is always youthful, just as eternal as the youthfulness of God."[27] We need to guide them in the ways of holiness now. To ensure youth's continued participation in the Church in the future, they need to have involvement and participation in the Church now. Engebreston see a way to keep youth in the church, when she claims that "positive personal religious experiences are an important inhibitor of adolescent drift from the churches."[28] The role of youth ministry is to help the parish and the Church as a whole provide such experiences. "A challenge to ministers and religious educators is to provide ways, sacramental or otherwise, in which the fears and burdens of young people can be supported in an accepting community whose backbone is a sense of hope."[29] How to address this challenge and how to provide experiences of faith for postmodern youth will be the subject of Chapter 6 below.

To return to the thesis statement, we focus on the person of the youth minister. "Faithful mission practice requires an understanding of the culture in which one is serving."[30] The youth minister needs a thorough understanding of postmodern culture before planning events and experienc-

27. John Paul II, "Evening Vigil," §6.

28. Engebretson, "Young People," 9.

29. Ibid., 14.

30. Gibbs and Bolger, *Emerging Churches*, 17.

es within the comprehensive model of youth ministry. The youth minister should not be afraid of this culture, it is the basic identity of the youth with whom they are ministering. "We need to be people who point to the positive potential of the present, who are not driven to despair by postmodern antiques, but who are able to affirm and develop those aspects of our lives and world that remain life-giving and life-sustaining."[31] Many of us involved in youth ministry are members and/or products of postmodernism. Jones summarizes the situation:

> Those of us who are Gen-Xers are the cusp generation. In college, our parents and the Boomers studied under post-Enlightenment, modern professors. We studied during the transition. But the Millennials are getting full-blown, no-holds-barred postmodern thought . . . the students with whom we work were born into a culture in transition, and children born today are entering a thoroughly postmodern world. This is not to say that all students will adopt postmodern traits, but postmodernism will be the reigning school of thought, and postmodernity will be the reigning culture when our students arrive at college.[32]

Even if the ministers are from an older generation, they can still draw on experiences of change and adaptation in their own lives to help them understand the postmodern generation.

---

31. Horell, "Fostering Hope," 28.

32. Jones, *Postmodern Youth Ministry*, 29.

In the *Emerging Church*, Gibbs and Bolger found that "a desire for a holistic spirituality filled the culture, but the church found itself ill prepared for the task."[33] This is not a point about which Catholic ministers should despair, as other churches were just as ill prepared. The next chapter examines some of the different attempts by various faith traditions to adapt the Gospel message to postmodern culture. They are all based on churches and ministers trying to understand the postmodern mindset and the unique demands that ministry with postmodernists entails.

33. Gibbs and Bolger, *Emerging Churches*, 88.

5

Postmodern Youth Ministry
Part I: Learn From Our Experiments

How do we effectively minister to postmodern youth? What do we do with postmodernism? We should by this point begin to see that it is not a fad that will quickly go away. Nor should we blindly follow its tenets. "Postmodern theory has been circulating among universities since the early 1970s, but has only recently reached the attention of mainstream youth workers who have begun to ask, 'What is postmodernity's significance—is it a problem to be solved, a distortion to be resisted, a welcome source of methodological insight, or more cynically, simply the latest fashion?'"[1] Over the past forty years, there have been many attempts to incorporate postmodern theory in youth ministry; some successful, some not. This section examines those attempts that were not as effective as others. One of the major flaws in the failed attempts is the allowance for the complete adaptation of the Gospel itself to the postmodern ideals. The core beliefs of the church were sacrificed to keep postmodern youth in the church. Completely surrendering the identity of church to a particular culture is not effective. Faithful mission practice needs to retain the hallmarks of the church

1. White, "Illusions," 7.

and the faith as it tries to adapt the message to new listeners and new cultures. Realizing the errors of complete acquiescence to a culture, other faith traditions have studied ways to work with postmodern youth culture while maintaining their identity and beliefs.

This will be a good place to pause and speak about this concept of youth minister as missionary. This point is greatly emphasized by Jones[2], but with conflicting theories. I disagree with his statement that:

> A missionary . . . comes to her mission field with the express intent of *rocking the boat*. A missionary comes to challenge the reigning paradigms, to teach a new way. A missionary cries into the wilderness of six billion people, 'Repent of your old ways! Do not marry the reigning culture! Look upon everything you do with fresh eyes, with a new pair of lenses. Take *nothing* for granted!' A missionary dives into culture headfirst and swims around, learning, perceiving, and discerning.[3]

This is the wrong idea for a missionary, that you have all of the answers and can fix everything wrong with them. At Glenmary Farm in Vanceburg, KY, the farm managers remind our student volunteers that the people of Lewis County were fine before we got there and will be fine when we leave.[4] The mission trip is about learning and sharing with a new culture. Jones also speaks about blending into the mission territory, specifically by wearing the native clothing. So

2. Jones, *Postmodern Youth Ministry*, 46, 62.

3. Ibid., 69.

4. Glenmary, "Lewis County Facts," para. 7.

in youth ministry "we may take on some of the apparel of our students and their culture."[5] While this certainly has worked through the centuries, with great examples in Matteo Ricci in China and Roberto de Nobili in India[6], it is not strictly necessary and could be harmful with teens. Kids can spot a poser quite quickly. Presently at thirty-four years old, I would look like a fool in current teen fashion. While the students sometimes good-naturedly mock my conservative fashion sense (or lack thereof), it is not my clothing that is important, but my presence in their lives.

Theories of missionary activity will continue to be debated. Philip Jenkins in his history of non-western Christianity agrees that "churches must adapt, but they face the grave dilemma of just how far to take such accommodation . . . too little adaptation means irrelevance; too much leads to assimilation and, often, disappearance."[7] Being true to the postmodern feel of this study, two conflicting illustrations are appropriate. CNN Vatican Analyst and NCR journalist John Allen presents the "con" position, after speaking with some "Vatican officials:" "Theological movements trumpeting 'inculturation' threaten to produce a kind of weak Catholicism, in which the only thing really uniting Catholics is the name. The experience of the faith, its content and modes of expression, fragment to the point of being unrecognizable, especially in places such as Africa and Asia."[8] While the positive aspects of inculturation are advocated by Archbishop-emeritus Peter Sarpong of Kumasi,

---

5. Jones, *Postmodern Youth Ministry*, 79.

6. Gonzalez, *The Story of Christianity*, 406–8.

7. Jenkins, *The Lost History*, 245.

8. Allen, *All the Pope's Men*, 200.

Ghana, who actually prefers the word "inculturation" as opposed to "adaptation" or "translation".[9] Inculturation, for Sarpong, has fewer connotations of colonialism and having a European model forced onto a people; ignoring the fact that the faith came from an Aramaic-Hellenistic background, is an international church, and the European way is not the only way. For our study, we keep in mind that the truth of the Gospel remains unchanged, but the way we present it is material for discussion.

One of the greatest mistakes of early attempts at postmodern youth ministry was to simply create a separate church-within-a-church. If the main church service does not speak to the youth, some churches have a separate service for the youth. This situation is not the same as having a separate Sunday school or other religious education programs differentiated by age. What is taking place is a separate worship service every Sunday. The youth pastor becomes the only minister the youth will see and the other youth are their only experience of a congregation, with even the parents of the youth separated from them. While the minister is able to focus specifically on what will speak to youth in a worship service, the flaw is that this is not true church. Gibbs and Bolger's experience showed them that "A church-within-a-church does not challenge the autonomy of the individual."[10] Youth are only surrounded by other youth. It is reminiscent of the way the media as a whole caters to youth culture. It furthers the self-absorption of this age of development and negates any challenges for growth. This model can continue past the teenage years

9. Sarpong, *Peoples Differ*, 21–37.

10. Gibbs and Bolger, *Emerging Churches*, 93.

as the group forms a separate young adult service as well. "Most churches-within-a-church and young adult services" are "preservationist, youth-church models aimed at retaining young adults in the life of the mother church."[11] It began with the best of intentions; a way to keep the youth in the church. With time, however, the congregation can become a grouping of different age and cultural groups sharing a building, but not truly worshiping together. As our other Christian worshipping communities have realized, "The young-adult-service approach to church doesn't really work . . . it lasts about four years and then gets taken over, blows up, or the emerging pastor gets fired due to conflict in values and philosophy of ministry."[12]

A similar situation can be seen in the Catholic Church particularly in the melting pot of the United States. With many cultures and language groups coming together to worship at the Mass within this international church, the challenge for liturgists and pastors is to have a service that speaks to the most intimate, spiritual heart of each believer. The goal is to achieve "church" as St. Paul taught: "As a body is one though it has many parts, and all the parts of the one body, though many, are one body, so also Christ. For in one Spirit we were all baptized into one body, whether Jews or Greeks, slaves or free persons, and we were all given to drink of one Spirit." (1 Cor 12:12–13). It is difficult to be one church and express our unity and one-ness in a large city parish with multiple language groups at separate Masses, but that is a challenge that must be faced.

11. Ibid., 33.
12. Ibid.

A similar problem, and more closely representative of our study, might be found in the LifeTeen program. LifeTeen is a youth ministry program centered around contemporary, youth-oriented Eucharistic celebrations with music, decoration, and preaching geared towards youth culture. A LifeTeen Mass orients everything to the language and custom of the youth of the parish. The danger is if this became the Catholic version of a church-within-a-church that some evangelical churches have warned us about, yet a balance to this problem could be brought by inviting all parishioners to participate in the LifeTeen Mass or making one of the regular Sunday masses the LifeTeen Mass. I believe LifeTeen can be a wonderful and life-giving program with fewer problems than an independent church, as LifeTeen always recognizes its membership in the international Roman Catholic Church; yet problems could still exist. This section is meant to bring up the question of cultural inclusion at the Mass, yet each diocese and parish will have to answer this for themselves.

We can see large church services on television and in our neighborhoods with light shows and large screens projecting the words to the songs. The use of technology in worship is becoming more and more a reality and we must be careful with how it is used. Our youth are more familiar with technology than previous generations. Technological advances are hallmarks of the Modern Age and continue through the Postmodern, but postmodernists need more than just a text displayed on an overhead projector. "A projected sermon outline with PowerPoint bullets is nothing more than boardroom modernity in electronic form."[13] The

13. Carson, *Transforming Worship*, 31.

demands of postmodernism require technology alongside the mystical, where powerful images and inspirational messages are displayed along with moving, appropriate music. We might be impressed with the work that went into such a presentation, but for most of our youth, it is not that complicated. As an example, Timothy Carson relates a conversation between a college student and her pastor: "You feel that you have to impress us with a trendy outline? I don't come to church for that."[14] It is not about the technology; it is about the message and the faith being imparted through the medium. We still need to learn the technology, though. As they are not impressed by its use, they will still notice its absence or even laugh at outdated uses. We also do not want to be guilty of pulling a "bait and switch" on our youth. We should never be afraid to proclaim who we are and in what we believe. Contemporary music, PowerPoints, and laser shows, can all be used as tools towards spiritual growth, but the content should be honestly Christian from the first. We should not market a rock concert on its own when it is actually a church service. "Students will not respect us if we lure them in with secular music and movie clips, and then a year later in small group they find out that we only want them listening to Christian music and watching *Veggie Tales*! We must be vigilant and look out for those things that might threaten the integrity of our ministries."[15] We should never cave into the temptation that the ends justify the means and hide our message to get the teens to show up for the first meeting. This is lying and sinful.

14. Ibid., 70.
15. Jones, *Postmodern Youth Ministry*, 87.

Other faith traditions have also learned the necessity of the centrality of faith and the secondary nature of modern technology. The Modern Age was guided by reason and many churches were concerned with presenting the faith in a reasonable manner. The churches leading the charge into postmodern territory were quick to abandon reason and focus again on the other-worldly. They looked around for those practices that would best create an experience of the holy and their gaze fell on the higher tradition churches that never really fell under the sway of modernism in the first place. Scott Bader-Saye, in "The Emergent Matrix," shares that "the emergent church is not shy about raiding the storehouses of the Roman Catholics, the Orthodox, and the Anglicans for richer liturgies as well as prayer such as prayer beads, icons, spiritual direction, *lectio divina*, and a deeper sacramentality."[16] In line with Thomas Keating's Centering Prayer retreats, the Catholic Church is glad to open its wealth of experience in prayer to others, but a problem occurs in that these churches are borrowing only the external expressions of a theology that they do not exactly share or understand within the continuity of tradition. While the base belief in Jesus Christ is present, these churches are expressing a sacramentality without a belief in the Sacraments or a sacramental imagination.[17] These churches are borrowing practices based on how they fit a particular need, not out of an interior movement of discernment. Pastor Robert Webber shares his concerns with this problem in a conversation with Bader-Saye, "I think the major problem is that you may be rediscovering the ancient

16. Bader-Saye, "The Emergent Matrix," 21.
17. Cf. Greeley, *The Catholic Imagination*.

as a new gimmick. If you don't do the theological thinking that stands behind liturgy and sacrament and all the kinds of things that are part and parcel of the classical tradition, this will just fade out."[18] It is not just about mimicking what seems to work for others; it is about being in touch with the core beliefs of your faith and expressing this in terms that will best speak to postmodern culture. It is a fine line to walk. "How is this closer relationship between church and youth possible without thinking and working in terms of adaptation?"[19] Roebben is not speaking of adaptation in the same way that I am referring to it in this thesis. He is referring to the danger of adapting the church itself completely to the cultural ideals of postmodernism. This is a dangerous evangelization theory in that the attempt to gain members for a church causes the church to stop being a church at all. Couchman warns us that "There's a real temptation to dilute the message to make it fit in with contemporary feelings."[20] David White also points this out in a self-study for today's youth ministers: "Consider how often in the practice of youth ministry, we find ourselves rushing to embrace each new gimmick—new media devices, computerized broadcast capabilities, newest games, etc. in order to avoid being thought of, whether by youth or other youth workers, as 'out of style.'"[21] I am personally a gamer. I enjoy video games and discussing strategies with my brother. I can also discuss this with my youth, not in an attempt to appear relevant, but in an honest sharing of interests. At the same time, I

18. Bader-Saye, "The Emergent Matrix," 22.

19. Roebben, "Shaping a Playground," 342.

20. Couchman, "Understanding the Times," 49.

21. White, "Illusions," 24.

view these discussions as teachable moments on the topics of violence and the obsession and isolation that can come from abuse of the games. I did not start playing games to attract youth to my programs, I have been there since the first Atari. White continues by warning us that "there lies within the culture of professional youth ministry a gravitational force that compels us to embrace each new fad. Currently, the temptation is great to fashion our youth programs to fit prominent versions of postmodern."[22] This thesis calls for an understanding of the culture and a call to adapt the message to culture, but not to dilute the message into less than it is.

Pastor Webber continues his critique of failed attempts in that "contemporary worship" and "seeker services" looked like "Christian versions of rock concerts."[23] He complains about the "rah-rah youth movement" that is based on "feelings and loudness . . . as if the louder you can be, the more direct relationship you have with God. There's nothing here in the public face that lifts you theologically or lifts you into liturgy or anything that has historic connection or depth or substance."[24] The church service has become a rock concert completely. There may be much calling of the name of Jesus, but little reality of the message he preached. In much the same vein, Tony Jones also warns about what he has heard as the "emotional rape"[25]of our teens. This can happen on longer retreats, youth rallies, mission trips, and revivals. It is where we work up our students into an emo-

22. Ibid.

23. Bader-Saye, "The Emergent Matrix," 24.

24. Ibid., 20.

25. Jones, *Postmodern Youth Ministry*, 131.

tional whirlwind where they love Jesus more than anything and have a deeply moving conversion experience, and then we drive them home and leave it at that. Large events can be wonderful tools in our ministry, but only as a part of the daily grind of relationships. We cannot have emotion without catechesis and we cannot attack our students' emotions without the continued care of our on-going presence and ministry. These powerful experiences can also produce a distaste for home and the parish unless we can moderate discussions about the event and how the teens can incorporate their feelings into their daily life.

Much of these practices are based on the attempt to keep young people in the church. The problem with these attempts is that they are grounded in a mistaken theology of mission. The situation is spoken of in terms of either bringing youth into the church or going out into the world of youth to meet them on their turf. Both of these attempts fail to realize the reality that many youth are already in the church and that there is a distinct culture of youth, not a separate world. They are dealing with the same world we are, just with a different cultural and developmental lens. The challenge of figuring out ways to bring youth into the church or ways to go out into the world of youth, as Roebben shares: "are both based on the assumption that the relationship between church and youth can be expressed in terms of 'inside' and 'outside,' and that the efficiency of the strategy depends upon how one is willing to bridge the gap: by welcoming youth into the church or by going out to encounter them in the real world."[26] The mission of the church is not about bringing others over the bridge of difference

26. Roebben, "Shaping a Playground," 342.

into the church, it is to move together across the bridge of time towards the fulfillment of the Kingdom. Youth are a blessing for the Church and should not be treated as a problem to be solved or a phase to be endured. Arthur Canales, when speaking in agreement with Pope John Paul II, claims that "the old adage, 'the youth are the future of the Church,' is rubbish; the pope recognizes that the youth *are* the church—*right now*—today, contributing members through their baptismal call."[27] Every attempt must be made to help youth through this developmental time, acknowledge their unique cultural identity, while at the same time creating space within the existing worshipping community. The existing community does not abandon its identity, or else its mission is a lie to the youth it is trying to keep. "The youth ministry will be only as successful insofar as it is faithful: faithful to its youth, faithful to its mission, and faithful to the Gospel."[28] Faithful mission to postmodern youth should be modeled after the ministry of St. Paul who became all things to all people, without watering-down the demands of the Gospel. (1 Cor 9:19–23). Paul's mission embraced new cultures, as should our own. "Youth ministry should engage in ongoing dialogue . . . its aim is not to bring young people to the church or to bring the church to young people."[29] The aim is to *be* church *with* the young people.

27. Canales, "Models," 210.

28. Ibid., 230.

29. Roebben, "Shaping a Playground," 345.

6

Postmodern Youth Ministry
Part II: Pastoral Applications

AFTER EXAMINING these *attempts* at postmodern youth ministry, we now focus on some suggested methods for *effective* postmodern youth ministry. We take into account the mistakes made in the previous section, the goals of youth ministry from *Renewing the Vision*, and what we have learned about postmodern youth to create a framework for ministry. This chapter hopes to lay the groundwork for a more comprehensive model or study for the future, but with ideas for the working youth minister to begin implementing today. Just as in the chapter on Postmodern Youth, the pastoral ideas begin with the results from the 1996 survey by Roland Martinson. Martinson here describes the data on young adults who have remained active in the church and the reasons they have stayed. "Among the 25 percent who have stayed involved in the church, we have discovered varying combinations of eight characteristics:

- Faith was deep in the identity and practices of their family.

- Mentors: significant relationships with leaders whose faith is a vital part of their own lives. (Generally, they have three or more of such faith-filled leaders).

- Service in the name of Christ

- Being apprenticed into leadership early

- Having a safe and open place during their senior high and college years to ask tough questions, be in relationships with other persons like themselves

- Worship: an engaging intersection of the gospel with their lives

- Friends from a faith community who invite them to worship, Bible study, or support groups

- Christian community support during times of transition or crisis."[1]

Using these results throughout this section, we can begin examining the different facets of the beginnings of postmodern youth ministry.

For youth to belong to a parish, they must feel they truly do have a place in the parish. They are not a separate "youth group" who run bake sales and wash our cars, nor are they a confirmation class that gathers once a year and then is ignored. In response to the postmodern need for community, *Renewing the Vision* states that: "Young people should feel a sense of belonging and acceptance as full-fledged members of the community. Young people are more likely to gain a sense of identity in the community if they are regarded as full-fledged members. If parishes are to be worthy of the loyalty and active participation of youth, they will need to become 'youth-friendly' communities in

1. Martinson, "Spiritual But Not Religious," data throughout article.

which youth have a conspicuous presence in parish life."[2] Youth must be welcomed as equal members of the parish and accepted just as they are. The teenage years are not to be endured but celebrated. The parish as a whole, under the supervision and inspiration of the coordinator of the comprehensive youth ministry program, must be a place where the youth can truly feel at home. They need to be comfortable being who they are in this time of self-discovery. Youth ministry must become what Roebben calls the "playground for the transcendent."[3] The playground is the place for youth to safely experiment with different theories about how the world should be, what roles/vocations they can fill, and how far they are allowed to rebel as they figure out what they truly believe. The playground monitors accept the youth as they are: no discussion is taboo, no possibility is dismissed, and what is important to the youth is considered important. The monitors keep the youth within bounds, but allow them room to grow within. The parish needs to be a place of support and an arena to ask the tough questions of life, with caring adults and peers to walk with them as they search for the answers. The youth minister never dismisses a question as inappropriate to ask, yet stays on the journey of discovery with the youth. The journey helps the youth see that some questions must be "lived" in order to be understood. It follows the advice of Rainer Maria Rilke in the fourth letter of his *Letters to a Young Poet*.

> You are so young; you stand before beginnings.
> I would like to beg of you, dear friend, as well

2. U.S. Bishops, *Renewing the Vision*, 13.
3. Roebben, "Shaping a Playground."

as I can, to have patience with everything that remains unsolved in your heart. Try to love the *questions themselves*, like locked rooms and like books written in a foreign language. Do not now look for the answers. They cannot now be given to you because you could not live them. It is a question of experiencing everything. At present you need to *live* the question.[4]

By not giving a quick, canned answer and respecting the journey, the youth are more likely to see the parish as a place for *life-long* discovery and guidance.

It is with the liturgy that we see many of the issues of postmodernism played out. Modernism emphasized the rational over the mystical. "Modernism tells us that worship isn't necessary because we can figure it all out for ourselves through reason."[5] Worship can answer some of the questions that were raised by bringing enlightenment to those that are "spiritual, but not religious": providing an experience of the holy, filling up the lack of a metanarrative, and meeting the need for community. These aspects of postmodernism will be answered throughout each of the explanations below.

Worship addresses those that state that they are "spiritual, but not religious." They claim, according to Kelley, that they can pray at home and do not need a church or other people to have a relationship with God. "We can encounter God just fine by ourselves. While postmodernism doesn't deny that one can and should have significant individual encounters with the Lord, having those encounters in a

---

4. Rilke, *Letters*, 35.

5. Kelley, "An Introduction to Postmodernism," para. 21.

community setting is equally as important . . . they can learn from other people's experiences and insights into the divine."[6] While it is possible to be in a personal relationship with God and that we all need to cultivate such a relationship, God did not intend us to live our faith life without community. The postmodern youth will make claims to living it on their own, but will be much more thankful and vibrant in their faith life if given communal worship experiences. This in turn will create more communal and faithful individuals, according to the concept of "*lex orandi, lex credendi.*" In it, Prosper of Aquitaine teaches that "The law of prayer is the law of faith: the Church believes as she prays."[7] How we pray; the words, the physical posture, and environment we use; affect what and how we believe. Perhaps the emphasis should be even more on the side of the postures and actions we perform in prayer, for "just as nonverbal cues constitute three-quarters of the way human beings communicate, so the words of Christian faith are only a part of our entire language system."[8] For this to be affective, these communal worship experiences must be in the language of the postmodern culture. "For the church of the postmodern time this includes the reintroduction of nonrational categories of knowing—the ineffable, mysterious, and awe-inspiring— back into our worship."[9] This should not be as difficult for a minister in the Catholic Church, as we have always had the mysterious "smell and bells" that other churches are borrowing to combat modernist worship. Youth ministers

6. Ibid.

7. *Catechism*, 318, §1124.

8. Jones, *Postmodern Youth Ministry*, 150.

9. Carson, *Transforming Worship*, 26.

choose recognizable images and carefully plan all aspects of the liturgy to meet the goals of the message, the season, the feast, and the demands of postmodern culture. Eucharistic Liturgies should be steeped in symbolism where images and the symbols should be allowed to speak for themselves. "In the same way that a joke is ruined if you have to explain the punch line, so the power symbol carries its own impact and is often undermined by undue explanation."[10] Of course the understanding of the symbol also depends on the stage of adolescent development for the present students. Juniors and Seniors may be quicker to understand the symbolism, while my Sophomores have needed more discussion and sharing time to get the point.

For many, it is the experience that plants the seeds of faith. Whether it was a Christian they met, something they read in the Bible, or a worship service someone invited them to; the basis of the Christian faith is an experience of Jesus Christ. It is key to provide for this experience, more than going into the specifics of the message at first. The roots of this necessity are seen in Smith: "A large number of Christians have told me that the first time they entered a church they 'felt' something (which later they were able to describe as God's love or the Holy Spirit). Their faith began before they ever heard the 'facts,' and it began with a feeling."[11] It is not the situation, though, according to Carson, where we should *never* explain the symbols. "Periodic teaching on the meaning of, say, baptism or the Lord's Supper is essential. In the moment of celebration, however, we must allow seekers, and practicing Christians alike to be confronted by the

10. Ibid., 29.
11. Smith, *The End of World*, 105.

transcendent beyond in their midst."[12] Postmoderns want objective teaching along with experience. This experience of the transcendent will show those that are spiritual just how much spirit can be found within religion.

In her history of the building of St. Peter's in Rome, R. A. Scotti gives a summary which goes to the heart of why I continue to focus so much on the Catholic perspective of prayer, aside from I own personal beliefs. Speaking about Bernini's design for St. Peter's and Baroque art in general, Scotti posits the claim that:

> Religion is illusion. No institution understands that more profoundly than the Church of Rome. More than tenets and ethics, religion is mystery and magic, the ultimate conjuring act, body and blood from bread and wine. And the gleam of gold, the clouds of incense, the remote elevated person of the pope, the sacred art and evocative music, create that illusion. Stripped bare of all but its dogma, it would be exponentially reduced. Just as religious belief requires both reasoned argument and a leap of faith, so its practice requires both truth and illusion. Rarely, if ever, can the spirit be reached and released by intellect or engineering alone. Religious faith comes through the heart to the head. It causes sinners to repent, the proud to humble themselves, and the powerful to bow to a higher authority. Emotions and imagination make zealots, saints, and martyrs out of clay-footed mortals.[13]

12. Carson, *Transforming Worship*, 30.
13. Scotti, *Basilica*, 246–47.

This is why I believe the Catholic Church is perfectly positioned to lead ministry education for the postmodern generation and why so many other faiths borrow its practices. The Modern use of reason and theology coupled with the mystical sense of worship and ritual can be harmonized within the traditional practices of the Catholic Church.

For Catholics, a good place to see the interplay of symbolism, experience, and education is in the *Rite of Christian Initiation of Adults* (RCIA), the normal method for people to convert to Catholicism. The RCIA is designed around a journey, with sponsors who act as guides, a space (playground) to ask questions, experiences of the faith, and academic teaching on the doctrines of the faith. "Theologically, the RCIA is a liturgical and sacramental process that allows the seeker (catechumen or candidate) to experience God through the *rubrics* of the church's liturgy, the official *rites* that the church celebrates, and the *ritual* expressions that are typically found in Catholic Sunday worship around the world."[14] Youth ministers should borrow freely from the RCIA ideas to enhance their own understanding of the use of symbols and ongoing catechesis with their youth.

While the Eucharist is the source and summit of our lives in the Church[15] our youth need to be given experiences of the holy in prayer throughout life as well. While it is true that we pray within a community and need each other within this prayer, we all need personal prayer as well. We need to educate our youth on the different forms of prayer, to be used within our various communal gatherings as well as those they can use in private. The "spiritual, but not religious" will need

14. Canales, "Models," 217.

15. Flannery, *Vatican Council II*, 6.

ongoing personal experiences of prayer for them to see the truth of the existence of God and the necessity of a relationship with God. I believe that, along with the communal experiences, the postmodern hunger for community can be answered by this relationship with God. For postmodern youth, we should also look to past attempts in planning these prayer experiences. Kelley has seen that "many youth groups have abandoned spotlights, PowerPoint presentations, and electric guitars . . . in favor of candlelight, contemplative music or pure silence, and ancient spiritual disciplines such as *lectio divina*, Ignatian prayer, and Taize-style worship."[16] Again we see other faith traditions borrowing from the history of Catholic spirituality.

Two prayer forms in particular, *Lectio Divina* and Ignatian "Application of the Senses," help combat the postmodern destruction of the authority of the Bible by the loss of the metanarrative and the loss of objective truth. Smith believes that: "There is a way of allowing our minds to settle into the Bible, not to dissect, analyze, compare, and conclude, but simply to *be* with God's Word."[17] Delving into our history, as Thomas Keating inspires us to do, we can incorporate the method of *Lectio Divina*.[18] This prayer form of "Sacred Reading" focuses on the inspiration of the text of the Bible more than deconstructing it to get at truth. The truth of the text is seen through an experience of its efficacy in our own lives. The other method of subjective scripture study comes to us from St. Ignatius of Loyola and is popularly known as the "Application of the Senses." Within the

16. Kelley, "An Introduction to Postmodernism," para. 22.

17. Smith, *The End of World*, 114.

18. Cf. Pennington, *Lectio Divina*.

Spiritual Exercises, Ignatius provides a "method of prayer by which one deliberately tries to imagine particular sensual details (sounds, colors, etc.) of a Gospel or other scene in order to feel part of it in a reflective, contemplative way."[19] This method would work well with postmodern youth in that it bypasses any questions of the truth of the text or the historic facts of authorship and focuses on the experience of the texts within the heart of the prayer. The youth would be able to experience truth within the Bible and, with time, perhaps restore some form of a metanarrative by experiencing the continuous truth contained in the whole of scripture. As St. Ignatius and Fr. Pennington would agree, though, all of this should be done under the ongoing guidance of a spiritual mentor or guide, who most appropriately could be the pastor or the youth minister. The guide keeps one on the right track, is a sounding board for experiences, and provides grounding in the faith tradition. This guidance would also continue to answer the postmodern need for community and the proven efficacy of a mentor. In closing this subsection on worship and prayer, I suggest one further form of prayer for use with your postmodern youth. While it may seem either traditional or old-fashioned, teaching the rosary to your youth may reveal to you and to them that "simple mantra like repetition may internalize deep truths."[20]

The time we spend at Mass, the opening and closing prayers at meetings, and the opportunities for further prayer and direction within the comprehensive youth ministry program do not always provide enough time to teach

19. Ignatius, *Personal Writings*, xv.
20. Carson, *Transforming Worship*, 30.

methods of prayer, nor enough experiences of prayer to become habitual. Canales believes that: "Weekend retreats are the spiritual backbone of a quality parish-based youth ministry."[21] Retreats provide the opportunity for longer experiences of prayer for the "spiritual, but not religious," catechetical discussion groups on the meaning of the symbols used, group sharing within a "transcendent playground" model, Masses planned by and geared strictly towards youth, and surround the youth in the warmth of community which they so desire. The effective youth minister will take all of the individual pieces of postmodern youth ministry into account when planning the retreat, including using a planning team consisting of youth and adults.

One further word beyond the pieces already discussed; do not be afraid of including prayer methods and retreat formats that some might consider more "advanced." Completely silent, contemplative retreats can work with high school teens, as well as retreats in a monastery following the same schedule as the monks or nuns. While in Ghana on an immersion trip, we joined the brothers, nuns, and priests in Mass every morning at 6:30. Even in the midst of the culture shock and the tracking of our students on the other side of the world, time was still set aside for our most perfect prayer in the Eucharist; with practically no grumbling about the early time or from non-Catholics. I have also seen sixteen and seventeen-year-olds regularly practice Centering Prayer after I taught Keating's method to them on retreats. Carson considers the world in which our postmodern youth, as well as ourselves, now live: "Many young people today are drawn to silence, prayer, and contemplation. They long for a mys-

21. Canales, "Models," 211.

terious counterpoint to the white noise and speed of light information overload of their times."[22]

Retreats can take other forms beyond the self-contained. In addition to what has been said above about retreats and prayer, a pilgrimage can also battle the lack of metanarrative by getting the youth physically in touch with their spiritual heritage. While each group can consider the most appropriate site for it to visit, one of the most popular pilgrimage programs in the past twenty years has been the World Youth Days. While in Toronto in 2002, I recall Pope John Paul II reflecting on the history of World Youth Day and thinking about the initial impetus for the event. "I imagined the World Youth Days as a powerful moment in which the young people of the world could meet Christ, who is eternally young, and could learn from him how to be bearers of the Gospel to other young people."[23] Few moments in my life have been as moving as praying all night with over one million pilgrims and guests in an open field. The entire pilgrimage, as all should, included prayer, catechesis, history, faith experiences, community, and service.

A great example of service in terms of postmodern youth ministry with which I am most familiar would be the Christian Service Program at my own school, Archbishop Hoban High School. I have spoken about our program[24] and shared its components with numerous other schools, service coordinators, and campus ministers. In the program, all service must be performed in direct, face-to-face

22. Carson, *Transforming Worship*, 84.

23. John Paul II, "Evening Vigil," §1.

24. Archbishop Hoban High School, "Christian Service Program," #1.

ministry with the poor, underprivileged; i.e., soup kitch-
ens, homeless shelters, nursing homes, hospitals, tutoring
inner-city children, or working with the handicapped. The
purpose of the hours is to give the students an experience
of actual poor people by forming a relationship with them.
Hours are not counted if the student is behind-the-scenes
in a support ministry, such as sorting/sending clothes or
supplies to another location, as this does not provide a relationship for the students. Hoban's key to making judgments
on service sites is in the twenty-fifth chapter of the Gospel
of Matthew, where the Lord describes the type of work
done by his disciples. These include feeding the hungry,
giving drink to the thirsty, clothing the naked, and visiting
the sick and imprisoned. This service provides relationship
for the postmodern youth. It is a truth experience of the
realities of poverty and answers to the adolescent development question, "why should I help anybody else?" Roland
Martinson focuses on the "centrality of personal experience
. . . if they had experienced it, it was true . . . suffering is
especially seen as a test of genuine faith and truth."[25] The
suffering they see in the friends they have made in service
can point them towards this genuine faith and truth. It is
the youth minister's duty, according to *Renewing the Vision*,
"to provide concrete ways by which the demands, excite-
ment, and adventure of being a disciple of Jesus Christ can
be personally experienced by adolescents."[26] Service with
those that need it most should be a core component of any
postmodern youth ministry program.

---

25. Martinson, "Spiritual But Not Religious," para 9.
26. U.S. Bishops, *Renewing the Vision*, 11.

Within this world of ongoing service and ongoing mentorship, the same that we said in prayer can be stated here in service: sometimes there is not enough time in our youth's busy lives to keep up any significant service practice, or even to begin the habit of doing service. The youth minister is always concerned with providing experiences of prayer, retreats, vocational guidance, and service. Matt Kelley has found that "one of the most effective ways that many youth ministries do this is to take mission trips . . . teenagers come back from mission trips with a deeper faith commitment and a strong desire to serve God in their own communities. This fits in perfectly with postmodern attitudes."[27] Mission trips designed around a retreat model can answer the needs of an entire postmodern youth ministry program and can be a wonderful way to refocus and re-center the program each year.

The parish needs to provide room for the youth, but not just to minister *to* them; the parish ministers *with* them. The "Decree on the Apostolate of Lay People" of the Second Vatican Council teaches that "from the fact of their union with Christ the head flows the laymen's right and duty to be apostles."[28] Our teens are equal members of our parish by right of Baptism and, for many, the fullness of initiation in Confirmation. While participating in ministry as participants in the Mass, youth should be given additional opportunities for leadership and an equal voice at the table of parish discussion. The postmodern mind thinks in terms of consensus and demands to share in the discussion. Teens need opportunities for leadership development where they

27. Kelley, "An Introduction to Postmodernism," para. 17.

28. Flannery, *Vatican Council II*, 768.

can be prepared for future leadership and display their exist-ing talents for leadership now. Teens can be members of the parish council where they can be provided such leadership opportunities, along with other youth ministry programs. "In the Modern world, one tends to do things 'because Grandma did them'. In the Postmodern world, commit-ment is based on personal experience."[29] Postmodern youth will not sit by and watch as their futures are decided for them. They do not want to participate in activities in the parish because "this is what we have always done." Because of the disbelief in objective truth, they need to have an experience of something to know that it is true. This is in terms not only of parish activity, but all leadership oppor-tunities. This opportunity can best be explored within the comprehensive youth ministry plan. Every parish will have certain kids who want to be more involved, have the time to be involved, and enjoy each other enough to get involved. In the past, these kids were formed together as the parish "youth group." This worked well, but little was done beyond this group to reach the other youth in the parish. Now this group of core youth would join with the coordinator of youth ministry and other adults to form a Coordinating Team. The adults and youth together would plan the events for all the youth of the parish as well as advise the pastor on youth issues.[30] When planning for events involving post-modern youth, there should be an obvious necessity for having such youth around to help plan. "Today's youth are natives to postmodern culture while those of us from the

29. Wood, "Congregationalism," 75.

30. U.S. Bishops, *Renewing the Vision*, 44.

Baby Boom and earlier generations are immigrants."[31] The opportunities to display the leadership development within this group would flow over into the planning of the liturgy as well. It would be a place, again as in *Renewing the Vision*, that would "provide opportunities for young people to be trained as liturgical ministers, schedule periodic youth event liturgies that are prepared with young people's input and assistance, and invite young people to help prepare the community liturgies."[32] Youth can be involved in the planning of liturgies and in the ministries of the Mass. There should be teens on the regular rotation of lectors, extraordinary ministers of Holy Communion, music ministry, and the other roles at Mass. Having a role to play provides ownership and instills the sense that this is their parish as well.[33] Care should be especially taken when planning the music for Mass. *Renewing the Vision* teaches that "music is a significant part of personal expression for young people and that desire carries over to their participation in liturgy."[34] Young people should have a role in the planning of liturgical music as they will be the best guides as to what will speak to them, and to what they will actually sing. While the Mass should be planned in a way to speak to all cultures present, including postmodern youth, additional catechesis will always be required to explain the deeper meanings.

Before closing this discussion on postmodern youth ministry, an additional word needs to be said about the

31. Horell, "Fostering Hope," 29.

32. U.S. Bishops, *Renewing the Vision*, 44.

33. It would be interesting to study the statistics in the number of altar servers that became priests, or now lay ministers.

34. U.S. Bishops, *Renewing the Vision*, 46.

destruction of the metanarrative in postmodern culture. At the root of many problems for the youth minister is the fact that Christianity itself is a metanarrative. The ongoing Salvation History, the story of God's care and intervention in the drama of human history, is a metanarrative that explains much of who we are as Church and is the basis for all that we know and believe about our faith. One aspect of this faith that can be discussed with the youth is that throughout all of the transition and historic epochs of the past two thousand years, the Church remains. Our faith, our story, Engebreston believes, can be the basis to reintroduce the concept of an underlying, unifying story of human events. "In the face of postmodernism which is skeptical of all meta-stories, the redemption story of Christianity treated as an open narrative in dialogue with culture, can surely be used as the foundational underpinning of study of the ways in which human beings can, do and will in the future improve the world."[35] The key here is the "open narrative in dialogue with culture." Our youth should be given the opportunity to experience the faith, ask questions about the faith, and even doubt the faith. The truth of God can endure all doubts and can be eternally patient for our decision to follow Christ. It is God that has endured all of these changes throughout history and God that will continue to be there once the postmodern transition becomes the next epoch in time. "She [Wisdom], who is one, can do all things, and renews everything while herself perduring." (Wis 7:27).

Throughout all of these reflections on leadership development, worship, prayer, retreats, and service; the key has always been relationships. The point to youth ministry

35. Engebretson, "Young People," 21.

is to provide a space for youth to be who they are and guide them as they grow to what they are meant to be. "Growth in faith occurs within a communal context."[36] This is Church at its core, as *Gaudium et Spes* reminds us that "by his innermost nature man is a social being."[37] Our identity as being created in the image and likeness of God is shown in the nature of God as community, God as Trinity. Gibbs and Bolger firmly believe that: "To be church is to participate in the Trinity/divine life of God. Because God is the source of all relationality, to focus the church on relationships is to be Christian at the core."[38] By nature and by current circumstance, the postmodern youth desperately needs to be in relationship. With the break-up of the home and the lack of trust in society or any institution, they continually ask questions about fidelity. Martinson speaks up for youth with the question: "Will there be someone there with me, for me?"[39] It is the community as a whole, but in particular the person of the minister, that must be the one that is there for the youth.

THE PERSON OF THE YOUTH MINISTER

So much of this exploration has dealt with the history of the terminology, the identification of the characteristics of our subject, the history of the vocation, and negative and positive examples of postmodern youth ministry. It is here that I turn your attention to the person actually doing the minis-

36. Horan, "Youth Ministry," 29.
37. Flannery, *Vatican Council II*, 913.
38. Gibbs and Bolger, *Emerging Churches*, 102.
39. Martinson, "Spiritual But Not Religious," para. 49.

try. The coordinator of youth ministry in these postmodern times must first and foremost understand postmodernism. Smith claims that they "need to study postmodernism the same way missionaries immerse themselves in a foreign culture in order to effectively communicate the gospel."[40] This has been a thesis we have revisited numerous times. The youth minister must understand the history and doctrines of their faith tradition before facing the questions and doubts of those in their charge. This is not a job for a new volunteer that simply wants to play volleyball with youth of the parish once a month. This is a ministry and a vocation in the Church and must be discerned accordingly. They must be fully prepared to be the mentor that the postmodern youths need. The youth minister, for Engebreston, must make "a genuine attempt to enter into their {youth} experience and to travel with them in the religious issues that are arising in their lives . . . to respect their experience, identifying the religious questions that are on their minds, then acquainting them with the responses of religion to these questions."[41] The youth minister does not need to have all the answers, but must know the faith well enough to be able to walk beside the youth throughout this journey of faith. Youth ministers must be honest about their own beliefs and be prepared to question the flaws in modern as well as postmodern thought. "In order to uncover and answer postmodernism's dismissal of values . . . religious educators and youth ministers must help students to interrogate their own cultural conditioning, including the mind-

40. Smith, *The End of World*, 122.
41. Engebretson, "Young People," 19.

set of their own generation."[42] We do not blankly accept the postmodern culture in order to gain church members. We have objective truths that we have seen and come to believe. Youth ministers have arrived at a point on their faith journey where they have been called to minister to and guide others on the journey. They have seen the truth of the faith through experience themselves and it is now their duty to provide such experiences to the next generation. It is crucial for the youth minister to be honest about the journey of faith and the occurrences of doubt that accompany it. Ministers need "to bear witness to . . . this struggle with reality. Only when young people are confronted with adults who show the courage of this conviction, who live from the gospel in which they find 'enlightenment,' can religion be experienced as a valid option."[43] Youth need to see this experience of faith lived out in another, in an expert, who is not afraid to speak about their failings as well as their triumphs. The youth minister becomes the voice of truth because of experience and can lead the postmodern youth to an experience of Jesus Christ and faith in him as the ultimate truth.

---

42. Ibid., 23.

43. Roebben, "Shaping a Playground," 345.

Conclusion

Our study began with the reality of the waning of the Modern Age, a new historic epoch on its way, and the transitional period of postmodernism in which we find ourselves. We are faced with the challenge to communicate with the peoples of this new culture, postmodernism, in order to continue to spread the Gospel message. This is a challenge that *Gaudium et Spes* assures us we have the ability and the right to carry out: "It is possible to create in every country the possibility of expressing the message of Christ in suitable terms and to foster vital contact and exchange between the Church and different cultures."[1]

Youth ministers must have an understanding of this culture in order to work with it. It began with the Modern Age in the Enlightenment and Descartes, where the *cogito* placed human reason as the basis for all knowledge. Set on a search to discover what united humanity, all that made us different was cast aside. We looked for grand theories that explained the way things worked and placed great faith and the label of "truth" on what was discovered. There were rules and orders that governed everything and there was no limit to the achievement humanity could make on its own.

The Stock Market Crash of 1929, two World Wars, and the Holocaust led to the questioning of the unlimited progress humans can make left to themselves. Questions arose

1. Flannery, *Vatican Council II*, 946.

over the rules and laws that had made sense for so long. The old stories we told ourselves to make sense of the world no longer fit; so, many cast aside the stories. With the upheaval of the world in the 1960s, society began to deny all stories that tried to explain it all. We stopped believing that anyone could know the truth and we focused again on what made us unique and different. We would only believe something if we were able to experience it for ourselves. With the focus on personal experience and the continued charge of modern technology, the result was more and more a separation from each other and a life stuck in isolation and loneliness. With the downfall of reason, we tried to get in touch again with the otherworldly and the mysterious.

The effect postmodernism has had on our youth has been both a challenge and a blessing. Postmodern youth are more aware of minorities and technological advances. They have recognized the need for community and are less isolationists by choice, if not in reality. Yet they have lost any unifying story to explain the mysteries of the universe. Youth want to get in touch with the mystical, but will not believe anyone official that would know how to get there. Our youth are constantly after the next experience that will explain it all to them or make it more real, instead of trusting that what others are saying is true. At the same time they hunger for leadership, understanding, and community; the family structure has broken down through divorce and busier work schedules.

The history of youth ministry has been about recognizing the unique characteristics and needs that adolescent development presents in terms of faith formation. Many have tried to answer the needs of this new development in history, yet not all were effective or even appropriate. We cannot completely give up our identity and what we have come to see as true in order to appeal to postmodernism. Our youth might enjoy some aspects of the culture at present, but they are going to grow up eventually. The church that has transformed itself into something other than itself in order to attract youth might not be able to answer the needs of the young adults and new parents of a later age. Letting each age or cultural group have its own worship service goes against the unity we profess as Christians. The flash and glitz of a concert on its own do little to communicate the truths of the faith. They may attract participants, but these will leave once the music fades.

Effective Postmodern Youth Ministry adapts the Gospel message to postmodern culture while staying faithful to the Gospel itself. It does not water down the message to attract followers, but shows how the faith resonates within the deepest places of the postmodern youth's heart. It provides experiences of faith, prayer, worship, and service that let the youth see the truths of the faith. It creates a safe space for questioning, rebelling, and comfort. The emphasis is on the understanding and compassion of the youth minister. It is up to them to guide the rest of the parish in fulfilling what the youth truly need, for this faith is based not just on knowledge or a text. The Christian faith is based on an experience of our savior, Jesus Christ. As the Greeks requested of the apostles in John's Gospel, "we wish to see Jesus," (John 12:21) so too our youth are begging to have an experience of Jesus Christ, the core of our faith. This desire was the motivation for Pope John Paul II's Apostolic Letter about this new millennium, *Novo Millennio Ineunte*. "The men and women of our own day . . . ask believers not only to 'speak' of Christ, but in a certain sense to 'show' him to them. And is it not the Church's task to reflect the light of Christ in every historical period, to make his face shine also before the generations of the new millennium?"[2] It is the responsibility of the entire Church, under the guidance of the clergy and youth ministers, to let our youth truly see Jesus and so enter into the Kingdom of God.

At the center of our faith is our relationship with God. Bypassing postmodern objections to the existence of God, the truth of the revelation of Jesus Christ, the "myth" of the Biblical stories, and the corrupt history of religions; we always must return to this relationship. For it is through grace that we are saved. It is by grace that we can even begin to understand the mystery of God. For the story of God comes through grace, and even for the most strict of postmodernists, God's story must be listened to as equally as any other story. It will be through this opening, and prayers for continuing grace, that we can walk beside our teens on our path to salvation.

2. John Paul II, "*Novo Millennio*," §16.

Bibliography

Allen, John. *All the Pope's Men.* New York: Doubleday, 2004.

Archbishop Hoban High School "Christian Service Program Requirements," No pages. Online: http://www.hoban.org/s/1098 /images/editor_documents/200910%20School%20Year/ Campus%20Ministry/CHRISTIAN%20SERVICE%20 PROGRAM%20REQUIREMENTS%202009–10.pdf.

Bader-Saye, Scott. "The Emergent Matrix," *Christian Century* 121 (30 November 2004) 20–27.

Bainton, Roland H. *The Reformation of the Sixteenth Century.* Boston: Beacon, 1952.

Baker, Keith Michael, and Peter Hanns Reill, editors. *What's Left of Enlightenment? A Postmodern Question.* Stanford: Stanford University Press, 2001.

Borgmann, Albert. *Crossing the Postmodern Divide.* Chicago: University of Chicago Press, 1992.

Brown, Dan. *The DaVinci Code.* New York: Doubleday, 2003.

Brown, Raymond E. *An Introduction to the New Testament.* New York: Doubleday, 1997.

Canales, Arthur David. "Models for Adolescent Ministry: Exploring Eight Ecumenical Examples," *Religious Education* 2 (2006) 204–32.

Carson, Timothy L. *Transforming Worship.* St. Louis: Chalice, 2003.

Catechism of the Catholic Church. New York: Image/Doubleday, 1994.

Couchman, David. "Understanding the Times," *Evangel* 2 (2005) 47–53.

Descartes, Rene. *Meditations on First Philosophy.* Translated by Laurence J. Lafleur. Indianapolis: Liberal Arts, 1960.

Ehrman, Bart D. *A Brief Introduction to the New Testament.* New York: Oxford University Press, 2004.

Engebretson, Kathleen. "Young People, Culture, and Spirituality: Some Implications for Ministry," *Religious Education* 1 (2003) 5–24.

Erikson, Erik. *Childhood and Society.* New York: Norton, 1950.

Flannery, Austin, editor. *Vatican Council II: The Conciliar and Post Conciliar Documents.* Northport, NY: Costello, 1988.

Gibbs, Eddie, and Ryan K. Bolger. *Emerging Churches: Creating Christian Community in Postmodern Cultures.* Grand Rapids: Baker Academic, 2005.

Glenmary Farm Volunteer Program. "Lewis County Facts," No pages. Online: http://www.glenmary.org/farm/Volunteer_Information /Lewis_Co_Facts.htm.

Gonzalez, Justo L. *The Story of Christianity: Volume 1: The Early Church to the Dawn of the Reformation.* San Francisco: Harper Collins, 1984.

Greeley, Andrew. *The Catholic Imagination.* Berkeley: University of California Press, 2000.

Groothuis, Douglas. "Why Truth Matters Most: An Apologetic for Truth-Seeking in Postmodern Times," *Journal of The Evangelical Theological Society* Sept (2004): 441–54.

Hanawalt, Barbara A. *The Ties That Bound: Peasant Families in Medieval England.* Oxford: Oxford University Press, 1986.

Hebblethwaite, Peter. *Pope John XXIII.* Garden City, NY: Doubleday, 1985.

Henn, William. *The Hierarchy of Truths According to Yves Congar, OP.* Rome: Gregoriana, 1987.

Herlihy, David. "Medieval Children." In *Essays on Medieval Civilization*, edited by Bede Karl Lackner and Kenneth Roy Philp. Austin: University of Texas Press, 109–41.

Horan, Michael P. "Youth Ministry in a New Time: Building on the Past, Investing in the Future," *Theological Explorations: On-line Journal for Duquesne University Theology Department* I, 1: 29–35. No pages. Online: http://www.duq.edu/theology/_pdf/faculty-publications/theological-exploration1.pdf.

Horell, Harold D. "Fostering Hope: Christian Religious Education in a Postmodern Age," *Religious Education* 1 (2004): 5–22.

Ignatius of Loyola, Saint. *Personal Writings.* London: Penguin, 2004.

Inbody, Tyron. "Postmodernism: Intellectual Velcro Dragged Across Culture?" *Theology Today* 4 (1995): 523–37.

Jenkins, Philip. *The Lost History of Christianity: The Thousand-Year Golden Age of the Church in the Middle East, Africa, and Asia—and How It Died.* New York: HarperOne, 2008.

John Paul II. "Evening Vigil with Young People at 17th World Youth Day," 27 July 2002. The Vatican. No pages. Online: http://www.vatican.va /holy_father/john_paul_ii/speeches/2002 /july/documents/hf_jp -ii_spe_20020727_wyd-vigil-address_en.html.

John Paul II. "Apostolic Letter: *Novo Millennio Ineunte,*" 6 January 2001. The Vatican. No pages. Online: http://www.vatican.va/ holy_father/john_paul_ii/apost_letters/documents/hf_jp-ii_ apl_20010106_novo-millennio-ineunte_en.html.

Jones, Tony. *Postmodern Youth Ministry.* Grand Rapids: Zondervan, 2001.

Keating, Thomas. *Intimacy With God.* New York: Crossroad, 1998.

Kelley, Matt. "An Introduction to Postmodernism (And Why It's Not a Bad Word)," *Youthworker* (Nov/Dec 2003). No pages. Online: http: //www.youthspecialties.com/articles/topics/postmodernism /pomo_intro.php.

Martinson, Roland. "Spiritual But Not Religious: Reaching an Invisible Generation," *Currents in Theology and Mission* (October 2002). Database on-line. *FindArticles.* No pages. Online: http://findarticles.com/p/articles/mi_m0MDO/is_5_29/ai _93610956/?tag=content;col1

Nash, Robert J. "A Postmodern Reflection on Character Education: Coming of Age as a Moral Constructivist," In *Character Psychology and Character Education*, edited by Daniel K. Lapsley and F. Clark Power. 245–67. Notre Dame, IN: University of Notre Dame Press, 2005.

Nash, Jr., Robert N. *An 8-Track Church in a CD World: The Modern Church in the Postmodern World.* Macon, GA: Smyth & Helwys, 1997.

Neufeld, Tim. "Postmodern Models of Youth Ministry," *Direction* 31 (2002) 194–205.

O'Neil, Michael. "Ethics and Epistemology: Ecclesial Existence in a Postmodern Era," *Journal of Religious Ethics* 1 (2006) 21–40.

Pennington, Basil. *Lectio Divina.* New York: Doubleday, 1994.

Rilke, Rainer Maria. *Letters to a Young Poet*. San Rafael, CA: New World Library, 1992.

Roberts, Alexander, editor. *Ante-Nicene Fathers—Volume VIII*. In Early Church Fathers, edited by Phillip Schaff. Peadbody, MA: Hendrickson, 1994.

Roebben, Bert. "Shaping a Playground for the Transcendence: Postmodern Youth Ministry as a Radical Challenge," *Religious Education* 3 (1997) 332–47.

Rychlak, Joseph F. *The Human Image in Postmodern America*. Washington, DC: American Psychological Association, 2003.

Sarpong, Peter K. *Peoples Differ: An Approach to Inculturation in Evangelisation*, Legon, Accra-Ghana: Sub-Saharan, 2002.

Schneiders, Sandra M, IHM. *Finding the Treasure: Locating Catholic Religious Life in a New Ecclesial and Cultural Context*. Mahwah, NJ: Paulist, 2000.

Scotti, R. A. *Basilica: The Splendor and the Scandal: Building St. Peter's*. New York: Viking, 2006.

Segal, Daniel A. "'Western Civ' and the Staging of History in American Higher Education," *American Historical Review* 3 (2000) 770–803.

Singleton, Andrew, et al. "Spirituality in Adolescence and Young Adulthood: a Method for a Qualitative Study," *International Journal of Children's Spirituality* 3 (2004) 247–62.

Smith, Chuck, Jr. *The End of World . . . As We Know It*. Colorado Springs, CO: Waterbrook, 2001.

Solerno, Roger A. *Beyond the Enlightenment: Lives and Thoughts of Social Theorists*. Westport, CT: Praeger, 2004.

United States Conference of Catholic Bishops. *Renewing the Vision: A Framework for Youth Ministry*. Washington, DC: United States Conference of Catholic Bishops, 1997.

White, David F. "Illusions of Postmodern Youth Ministry," *The Journal of Youth Ministry* 1 (2007) 7–26.

Whitley, Rob. "Postmodernity and Mental Health," *Harvard Review of Psychiatry* 6 (2008) 352–64.

Wood, Joel Enoch. "Congregationalism E: Making the Way for Emergent Generations," *International Congregational Journal* 2 (2006) 65–83.